Dr. Marita Schauch BSc ND

# Collagen
## Myths & Misconceptions

### The Secret to Beautiful Skin, Strong Bones and More

ActNatural Corporation
5948 3rd Line RR#1
Hillsburgh, ON
N0B 1Z0

ISBN: 978-0-9867247-5-6

Copy Writing: Dr. Marita Schauch BSc ND
Copy Editing: Stephanie Bowen
Book and Cover Design: Jasper van Meurs

Printed in Canada by Friesens Corp.

# Life is a Gift.

*Never forget to enjoy and bask in every moment you are in.*

-Unknown

# Contents

# Foreword by Richard Passwater Jr.

The human body is a fascinating natural masterpiece of engineering. Its beauty is rivaled only by its strength and complicity.

Collagen is a structural protein that is a vital part of this engineering. Gram for gram, collagen's strength rivals that of steel. Its flexibility is far superior. I like to say collagen is the body's "go to" material to make whenever building something requiring both strength and flexibility.

The easiest place to observe collagen is in skin. Collagen provides elasticity and integrity; keeping the skin smooth, plump and supple. It's also what reflects light from the skin. A person's collagen content is a key factor whether he or she has a radiant, healthy looking youthful glow or a dull, gray appearance.

However, skin is certainly not the only place collagen has a critical job to do. In fact, collagen is the primary framework component of all connective tissue such as bones, tendons, ligaments, cartilage, and blood vessels. Its condition immensely impacts the functionality of all these tissues.

As an example, many modern bone researchers now believe that about 80% of bone strength is collagen dependent. Similarly, even modest collagen breakdown in joint tissue such as cartilage can be the difference between healthy and arthritic joints. And an increasing number of cardiovascular researchers are viewing collagen breakdown as a major reason for plaque formation in blood vessels. The biological pathways responsible for collagen production are very complex. Collagen-generating enzymes need to be activated in order to make new collagen. Unfortunately collagen-generating enzyme activity generally decreases as we age.

Over 100 years ago, Thomas Edison predicted *"The doctor of the future will give no medicine, but will interest his patients in the care of the human frame, in a proper diet, and in the cause and prevention of disease."*

In this book, Dr. Marita Schauch, ND delivers on Edison's prophesy. She does so by providing an enjoyable, yet comprehensive explanation why the quality and quantity of collagen impact both the strength and beauty of the entire human frame. In addition, she reviews many of the common reasons collagen production generally decreases as we age and discusses many common, but little known, factors that too frequently facilitate collagen breakdown and accelerate collagen loss.

Most importantly, Dr. Marita separates fact from fantasy by offering a well-researched, holistic plan of action. Her program consists of lifestyle and dietary advice, together with targeted supplement recommendations, to help protect existing collagen structures while also maximizing the natural production of healthy new collagen throughout the body.

I'm delighted Dr. Marita wrote this book. Whether somebody is interested in beauty or in other areas of health, I'm confident everybody reading this book will benefit learning some eye opening facts about how generating more collagen can make meaningful benefits to all connective tissues in the body and help them live a healthier and more rewarding life.

*To vibrant health and radiant skin,*
Richard Passwater, Jr.

# Acknowledgements

I would like to express my very great appreciation to my extended family at Preferred Nutrition and special thanks to my friend and mentor, Deane Parkes. Deane your wisdom and assistance is priceless. You've provided me with the platform to write and educate the masses; and for that, I am eternally grateful.

To my family and friends whose love and support provides me with the inspiration and passion to follow my dreams.

The love of my life, thank you for your patience and encouragement. I am so lucky to spend my life with you.

To my friend Nancy Cheeseman, I am so thankful for your encouragement, guidance and friendship.

I wish to acknowledge my friend and colleague Richard Passwater Jr. who has opened my eyes about the importance of collagen and helped me to understand its role in vibrant health.

My ND colleagues and friends of the health care field. Let's continue to support one another to heal, educate and create awareness about preventative medicine.

Finally, I would like to express my deepest gratitude to my patients. Everything I've learned over the years has come from listening and working with you! You have taught me, challenged me and shaped me into the doctor I am today.

# Introduction

## Don't Eat it – Generate it!

Collagen is one of those buzzwords – often heard, seldom understood. Leafing through beauty magazines, we see advertisements for "anti-wrinkle" creams and "serums," leading us to believe that all we need to do to increase the youth-preserving collagen in our skin is rub it on topically!

At the same time, *The American Society of Plastic Surgeons (ASPS)* reports that Americans spend $11 billion every year on face-lifts, Botox injections and other cosmetic procedures. But neither creams nor procedures do anything to help your body generate both health-improving and beauty-supporting collagen. That's right: *collagen doesn't just ward off wrinkles, it actually promotes health throughout the body.* This book will amaze you with the many things that collagen does to help us live strong, vibrant, and, yes, beautiful lives. By supplementing with key nutrients and maintaining a healthy diet and lifestyle, you will prevent the degradation of your body's stores of collagen. You'll also generate new collagen for the benefit of your entire body – not just the skin!

Some of the pioneers and authorities of collagen research include Professor Sam Shuster, Professor Andre Barel and Dr. Fuller Albright.

I was first introduced to the importance of collagen in the body from educator Richard Passwater Jr. I met him at a large national health food trade show, and people there – including me – were thronging to hear what he had to say. He was so passionate and his talk centered on many of the collagen-building nutrients, but the greatest of these was ch-OSA complex, a nutrient that has been scientifically proven to help the body generate its own collagen supplies. Much of what Richard has taught me about collagen is from his own research and learning from the above "godfathers" of collagen.

This miracle compound is available to all of us now, in the patented formula of **BioSil™**. Unlike most of the supplements that tout their ability to stimulate collagen production, this product doesn't break down in the digestive system. Activating specialized enzymes and partnering with additional nutrients such as lysine, and vitamin C, **BioSil™** goes deep. It actually turns on the switch to your body's own collagen-producing factories. It does this by activating enzymes your body naturally uses to make new collagen, making **BioSil™** one of the most bioavailable and effective products on the market. Indeed, a comparative study conducted by *The Journal of Parenteral and Enteral Nutrition* (1998) showed that the ch-OSA in **BioSil™** had the highest bioavailability when compared to horsetail and silica gel.

Having been in clinical practice for almost ten years, I can tell you that nothing I've used before has shown such vast – and fast! – results in my patients. Best of all, with **BioSil™**, the improvements to health and beauty come from the inside out – not the outside in (as with so many topical collagen treatments that promise a lot and deliver little). **BioSil™** is a wonder!

In this book, I'm happy to share with you everything I've learned about how to make this collagen innovation part of your healthier, happier, more youthful-looking lifestyle.

## CHAPTER ONE
# Collagen - The Body's Building Block

Collagen is the most abundant protein in the human body. It makes up about 25 to 35% of the body's protein content. It is often considered the "glue" that holds the whole body together.

Collagen fibers are long, straight, and unbranched, and are the strongest fibers in the connective tissue. Each collagen fiber consists of three fibrous protein subunits wound together like the strands of a rope. These fibers are called triple helix configurations, and, like a rope, they're very flexible, yet very strong when pulled from either end.

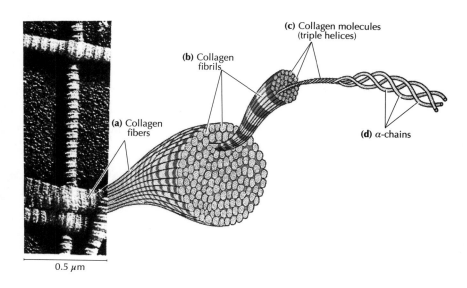

**(c)** Collagen molecules (triple helices)

**(b)** Collagen fibrils

**(a)** Collagen fibers

**(d)** α-chains

0.5 μm

# Where is Collagen Found? It's not just a Beauty Protein...

When we think of collagen, most of us are familiar with its role in healthy, beautiful-looking skin. But it doesn't stop there: collagen fibers are major building blocks in bone, joints (tendons and ligaments), and blood vessels (arteries and veins). In addition the quality and quantity of collagen in the skin help determine the health and beauty of hair and nails. Collagen is also found in the cornea of the eye, lining the gastrointestinal system, lungs, liver, kidneys, heart and the intervertebral discs.

To give you an even better idea of just how large a role collagen plays in our bodies, consider these percentages:
- **Skin** - 75% collagen
- **Bone** - 30% collagen
- **Joints**
  - Ligaments - up to 90% collagen
  - Tendons - 80% collagen
  - Cartilage - 70% collagen
- **Blood Vessels** - 40% collagen

Additionally, there are at least 28 different *kinds* of collagen that have been identified. The most common are:
- **Type I** – the most abundant collagen in the human body, found in the skin, artery walls, bones and teeth, tendons and ligaments. It's also present in scar tissue and helps with tissue repair.
- **Type II** – hyaline cartilage and also the cornea of the eye.
- **Type III** – blood vessels, spleen, lymph nodes, uterus, skin and intestines.
- **Type IV** – eye lens and kidney.

## Collagen Formation

The *fibroblast* is the cell in our bodies that is responsible for producing collagen. The formation of collagen is an intricate and complex chain of reactions that is dependent on specific vitamins and enzymes. Aging, stress, inflammation, poor diet, lack of exercise, and environmental toxins have a profound effect on the preservation of healthy collagen in the body.

The skin, for example, relies on ample collagen to prevent the absorption of toxins, pathogens and other microorganisms. Collagen is what helps with skin firmness and suppleness, and also regulates the renewal of skin cells. It is vital for skin elasticity. In fact, starting as early as age 21, collagen production in skin decreases about 1% per year, resulting in a decline in skin thickness and elasticity.

The collagen protein is made up of amino acids, which are in turn built of carbon, oxygen, nitrogen and hydrogen. Collagen generally contains 19 or 20 amino acids. 3 specific amino acids: L-Glycine, L-Proline, and L-Lysine are generally regarded as the most critical for collagen construction.

The synthesis of collagen starts with our body linking together amino acids in a specific sequence determined by our DNA. One of the first modifications to take place is a very critical step called *hydroxylation* of the selected proline and lysine amino acids in the newly synthesized chain to form hydroxyproline and hydroxylysine. Specific enzymes called hydroxylases are responsible for these important reactions needed to form hydroxyproline and hydroxylysine.

These hydroxylation reactions organize the chains in the conformation they need to form a triple helix. One of the ways **Bio-Sil™** works is by activating enzymes preforming this hydroxylation process. These hydroxylase enzymes also require Vitamin C; if a person is Vitamin C deficient, then this reaction will not occur.

In the absence of hydroxyproline, the collagen chains cannot form a proper helical structure, and the resultant molecule is weak and quickly destroyed. Poor wound healing can also occur.

You can see how complex the formation of collagen is, and how each amino acid is involved in each step, and highly dependent on the potent antioxidant Vitamin C.

## What is ch-OSA®?

ch-OSA® or *choline-stabilized orthosilicic* acid is a unique and highly bioavailable nutrient complex, clinically proven to activate the biological pathways that generate collagen in the body. Orthosilicic acid, or OSA, is a natural compound present in very dilute concentrations in mineral water and beverages such as beer. Unfortunately it loses its stability during bottling and processing, so don't go out and start drinking beer to improve collagen production!

A new technology has been developed to stabilize and concentrate OSA using choline, an essential nutrient your body needs to keep cell membranes functioning properly. Choline is a precursor of phospholipids, which are an essential component in all cell membranes. Choline is involved in cell signaling and nerve communication, lipid metabolism and also helps to reduce homocysteine - a collagen destroying compound commonly used as a marker linked to heart disease and chronic inflammation.

Beyond its ability to stabilize OSA, the choline component of ch-OSA® may bind to specific, cellular receptors for choline. As a result, ch-OSA® can enter target cells and activate biological pathways. Choline functions as a "transporter" of OSA into the target cells, and once in the cells the ch-OSA® starts generating your collagen.

ch-OSA® is the active ingredient found in **BioSil™**, clinically proven to generate collagen by activating your body's own collagen producing cells – your fibroblasts.

# CHAPTER TWO
# Collagen and Skin, Hair and Nails

The integumentary system is probably one of the most closely watched organ systems in terms of estimating the overall health of an individual. The integumentary system has two major components: the cutaneous membrane – **the skin**, and the accessory structures – **the hair and nails**.

When something goes wrong with the skin, the effects are immediately apparent. The skin can also mirror the general health of other systems, and many health care providers use the appearance of the skin (or even the hair and nails) to detect signs of underlying disease. The skin protects us from the outside world, cushions and protects the deeper tissues, excretes wastes, and regulates temperature. We also have sensory receptors in our skin, which provide the sensations of touch, pressure, temperature and pain.

## Our Skin – The Largest Organ in the Body

The skin of an average adult, if laid flat, would cover anywhere from 18 to 22 square feet. In contrast to the other body's organs the skin is nearly flat, with varying thickness. The thinnest skin is found on the eyelids, while the thickest is on the palms of the hands and the heels of the feet. The skin has two components: the superficial *epidermis* and the underlying connective tissues of the *dermis*. The epidermis is the protective outer layer, and the thicker dermis provides support and gives the skin both strength and suppleness.

The epidermis is multi-tiered. The outermost layer is called the stratum corneum, which is a sheet of dead skin cells that serves as a barrier against the outside world. Their number is considerable: some 30,000 to 40,000 dead skin cells are sloughed off every minute!

These cells originate in a lower region of the epidermis, the stratum basale, where new basal cells are generated. Fresh skin cells continuously shed cells, resulting in a new epidermis about once a month. There are also neighboring cells called Langerhans cells that scout for disease-causing intruders and other foreign substances. The epidermis also contains melanocytes, cells that make melanin, which give skin its color and protect it from the sun's UV rays.

Just beneath the epidermis is the dermis, the connective tissue that makes up the bulk of the skin. The dermis is often referred to as the "true skin" because it does not continually renew like the epidermis, and stays the same throughout life. The dermis contains blood and lymph vessels, nerve endings, hair follicles, sweat and sebaceous glands, and the proteins collagen and elastin.

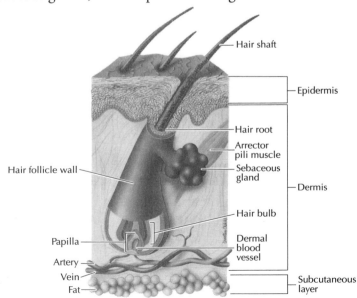

## Beautiful Skin Needs Collagen

Collagen in the dermis gives the skin its flexible strength; elastin enables the skin to return to its original shape when tugged and twisted. Beautiful, wrinkle-free skin depends on healthy production of collagen. In fact, skin consists of about 75% collagen!

Clinical studies have demonstrated the impressive role of choline stabilized orthosilicic acid (ch-OSA) found in **BioSil™** for healthy skin. In just 20 weeks, shallow wrinkles improved by 30% compared to the placebo group. Even more remarkable, skin elasticity measurements improved by 89% with the use of ch-OSA compared to use of a placebo. This was in women ages 40 to 65, who had clear signs of sun-damaged or prematurely aging skin.

**Reduced collagen causes skin to "cave in" and form wrinkles**

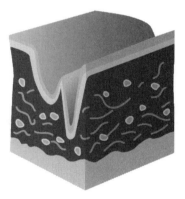

**Abudant collagen "pushes up & out" on skin, creating more youthful looking skin**

## Sun Exposure and Skin Aging

Ultraviolet (UV) light markedly accelerates aging by activating enzymes that break down collagen and elastin. The sun's UV rays also make skin rough and can over-stimulate pigment cells, causing unsightly age spots and skin cancer.

In the dermis, ultraviolet (UV) radiation causes collagen to break down at a higher rate than with just chronologic aging. Sunlight damages collagen fibers and causes the accumulation of abnormal elastin. When this sun-induced elastin accumulates, enzymes called *metalloproteinases* are produced in large quantities. Normally, metalloproteinases remodel sun-injured skin by reforming collagen. However in excess, these metalloproteinases can actually break down and destroy collagen. This results in the formation of disorganized collagen fibers known as solar scars. When the skin repeats this imperfect rebuilding process over and over again, wrinkles develop.

UV radiation in the skin can also result in the depletion of antioxidants such as vitamin E and vitamin C by targeting the epidermal layers. This extensively decreases the overall antioxidant capacity within the skin.

## Sugar and Glycation = Aging and Wrinkles

It is already well known that excess sugar in the diet can lead to a variety of health concerns, but what most individuals don't know is how negatively excess sugar can impact the health of our skin. When there is too much sugar in the body, protein molecules can link up with sugar molecules and create AGEs, or *advanced glycation* end products. Our body does not recognize these AGEs as normal, and as a result the immune system triggers an inflammatory reaction in the skin. Once these AGEs form they tend to gravitate toward the dermal layers of the skin, destroying collagen and elastin and resulting in wrinkling, loss of elasticity, stiffness, and accelerated aging.

The formation of AGEs has also been linked to the development of Alzheimer's, cardiovascular disease, diabetes and kidney disease.

## Hair

About five million hairs grow on the human body, with 100,000 found on the head. Hair plays an important role in protecting the scalp from the sun's ultraviolet rays and preventing heat loss. Eyelashes and eyebrows shield the eyes from the sun, foreign particles and perspiration.

Each hair shaft – the visible part – is actually a strand of dead tissue made up almost entirely of keratin proteins. Hair grows in follicles, or tube-like structures that originate in the dermis of the skin. At the base of the follicle is the hair bulb, where hair formation cells form new keratin. There is a portion of collagen rich dermal tissue (or dermal papilla) that is packed full of capillaries that project into the bottom of the bulb, providing nutrients to the cells and contributing to the health of the hair. So although hair is made from keratin, its health is highly dependent on having on adequate collagen.

## Hair Loss in Women

Hair loss (alopecia) is divided into two types: focal (small patches) or diffuse (all of the head). Diffuse hair loss is most often due to metabolic or hormonal stress, or to medications. It can vary from mild thinning to complete hair loss (from chemotherapy drugs). Focal hair loss is often secondary to an underlying disorder such as a fungal infection (tinea capitis) or an autoimmune disorder (alopecia areata).

Female-pattern hair loss is relatively common and affects approximately 30% of women before the age of 50. Common causes include excess testosterone, insulin resistance, polycystic ovarian syndrome, and low antioxidant status.

Free radical damage has also been shown to play a role in both female and male-pattern baldness. Higher levels of these damaging compounds are typically found in the hair follicles and accumulate due to lower levels of the antioxidant glutathione. An example of this free radical damage is the harmful and more potent form of testosterone, dihydrotestosterone (DHT), which is formed from testosterone by the action of the enzyme 5-alpha-reductase. The activity of this enzyme is increased in both male- and female-pattern hair loss.

A deficiency of specific nutrients can lead to hair loss in both men and women as well. Zinc, vitamin A, essential fatty acids, and iron are all important.

It's also well known that hair loss is one of the signs of hypothyroidism; therefore low thyroid is important to rule out as a condition for those women who suffer from thinning hair.

Believe it or not, the protein gluten that is found primarily in wheat, barley, and rye appears to create antibodies that can attack hair follicles, as well, thus acting as yet another cause of female-pattern hair loss. Avoiding gluten, especially if there are gastrointestinal symptoms (aka if you suffer from Celiac disease or a gluten intolerance) as well as the hair loss may be an important step for preventing further hair loss.

## Want Thick and Shiny Hair?

A big consideration for healthy hair and preventing hair loss is a unique nutrient complex called *choline-stabilized orthosilicic acid* (ch-OSA) found in **BioSil™**. Studies show that this highly bioavailable and stabilized form of silicon increases levels of *hydroxyproline*, a key amino acid required for the production of collagen and elastin. *Hydroxyproline* is used as a marker for healthy collagen synthesis. As you may have already guessed, these compounds are essential to the strength, thickness, and elasticity of hair. More col-

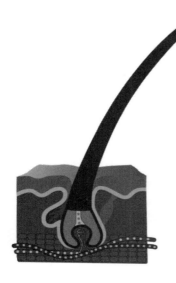

lagen in the dermal tissue also means greater blood flow to the hair, ensuring an abundant supply of growth-rich nutrients to the hair follicle. It is also believed that ch-OSA positively influences enzymes involved with forming keratin, the protein that makes up 97% of our hair.

To test the effects of this nutrient complex on women's hair, a randomized, double-blind, placebo-controlled study was conducted on 48 women with fine hair. Hair morphology and strength were evaluated before and after the treatment of 10 mg of silicon and 200 mg of choline as ch-OSA (or 2 **BioSil**™ capsules per day). Oral intake of ch-OSA had a positive effect on tensile strength including elasticity and break load, and resulted in thicker hair.

## Nails

Changes in the shape, structure, or appearance of the nails are clinically significant: a change may indicate the existence of disease affecting metabolism throughout the body.

Our nails are made up of several parts. The nail body is the most visible and also the hard part of the nail. It is a modification of the *stratum corneum*, or outer layer of epidermis. This translucent plate is composed of three tight layers of dead, keratinized cells that originate in the nail matrix. Besides containing keratin, the nail plate also includes trace elements (mainly iron, zinc, and calcium) and small amounts of lipids and water.

Nail growth begins in a part of the matrix called the nail root, an area of intense cell production. Healthy nails have a smooth upper surface, but vertical ridges may appear with aging. The nail plate appears pink from the dermal capillaries below, while clusters of new cells give the lunula (the "moon," or pale crescent) its white color.

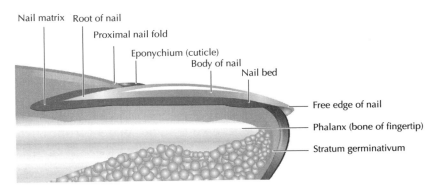

## Nails as Indicators of Illness

Many illnesses not only affect nail growth, but can cause disfiguring changes in the nails:

- Brittle, concave, spoon-shaped, or ridged nails may indicate an iron deficiency.
- Spoon-shaped nails or brittle nails can be an indicator of hypothyroidism or heart disease.
- Nails separating from the nail bed could be a sign of hyperthyroidism such as Graves' disease.
- Black marks under the nail plate could indicate respiratory or heart disease.
- Individuals with psoriasis or connective tissue disorders (Reiter's) often have "pitting" – small dents – in their nails.
- Yellow nails can be an indication of chronic bronchitis or other respiratory diseases.
- White spots can point to the need for vitamin B6 or zinc.
- Peeling nails may indicate low vitamin A, C or calcium.

## Banish Brittle Nails

Barring any disease, sometimes we have brittle nails simply because the nail matrix requires more collagen.

The nail matrix produces cells that eventually become the nail plate. The size, length, and thickness of the matrix determine the size, length, and thickness of the nail plate. The unique nutrient complex *choline-stabilized orthosilicic acid* (ch-OSA) found in **Bio-Sil™** amplifies the amount of collagen surrounding the nail matrix. More collagen in the dermis means greater blood flow to the nail matrix, ensuring an abundant supply of growth-rich nutrients to the nail. The increased blood flow also stimulates the production of keratin, the protein that makes up the majority of the nail plate.

In a study of Barel et al. (2005), the score for brittleness of hair and nails decreased significantly in the ch-OSA group, whereas no significant change was observed for women in the placebo group. After 20 weeks a significant decrease of nail brittleness was shown with 10 mg of silicon and 200 mg of choline as ch-OSA (or 2 **Bio-Sil™** capsules per day). **Remember to rule out any underlying diseases with your MD or ND with respect to nail health.

## Beauty from the Inside Out:
## Lifestyle and Diet Tips for Beautiful Skin, Hair and Nails

A diet full of nutritious and colorful food is an essential prescription for healthy and vibrant skin, hair and nails. The good news is that the foods that maintain beautiful and youthful skin are also excellent for your overall health.

While genetics can play a role in skin aging, poor lifestyle choices and your surrounding environment can significantly accelerate this process. Skin aging and damage typically occurs as a result of oxidation from free radicals. Free radicals are unstable molecules that can cause a lot of damage and inflammation in the body. As mentioned above, too much sugar can cause AGEs, which can damage your skin. Too much UV exposure and unhealthy habits such as smoking are also culprits in premature wrinkling and skin damage. Take some time to read chapter eight of this book, *Collagen and Environmental Toxins*, to familiarize yourself with strategies for further reducing free radical damage that can be incurred from many of the commodity items (makeup, cleaning products, etc.) we use every single day.

Aside from the above lifestyle changes, it's also important to include foods in your diet that are rich in antioxidants. Antioxidants work to protect your healthy cells, including your skin, hair and nail cells, against the damage from oxidative stress and free radicals. Some of these antioxidants include vitamin C, vitamin E, selenium, vitamin A (beta-carotene) and phytochemicals that are found in many excellent foods, as discussed below.

Vitamin C is a key player in the production of healthy collagen. It activates key enzymes in the collagen generating process and in addition, protects cells from free radical damage, boosts the immune system and helps to reduce inflammation. Good sources of vitamin C include broccoli, Brussels sprouts, bell peppers, mangoes, kiwi, oranges, pineapple, and papaya.

Vitamin E, another important antioxidant, helps to protect the skin from the sun's UV radiation. Great food sources of Vitamin E include sunflower seeds, almonds, spinach, Swiss chard, avocado and asparagus.

Vitamin A (beta carotene) is critical for healthy skin and is involved in the growth and repair of your body's tissues. Sweet potato, carrots, collard greens, winter squash, spinach and cantaloupe are excellent food sources of beta-carotene.

Selenium is an important antioxidant that protects the skin from sun damage. Selenium is required for the proper activity of enzymes called glutathione peroxidases. These enzymes play a key role in detoxification and protect against oxidative stress. Selenium-containing enzymes are also involved in recycling vitamin C, allowing for greater antioxidant protection. Food sources include sardines, Brazil nuts, lamb, chicken, mushrooms and eggs.

Omega-3 fatty acids, although not classified as antioxidants, have a significant role in protecting healthy skin. Omega-3s help maintain cell membranes, allowing water and nutrients in but keeping the toxins out. They are also very effective at reducing inflammation in the body, which is often the underlying cause of many chronic diseases. Clinical signs of essential fatty acid deficiency can include dry, scaly rashes; decreased growth in infants and children; increased susceptibility to infection; and poor wound healing. Neurological and visual development can also be impacted from an omega-3 deficiency. Dietary sources of omega-3s include flaxseeds, walnuts, sardines, salmon, herring and anchovies. To ensure a high concentration of omega-3s in the body, it's typically recommended to supplement with a clean, third party-tested fish oil in addition to dietary sources.

Clinical studies have also been conducted to show that certain natural polyphenols – plant chemicals that work as potent antioxidants – help to protect the skin against free radical damage. These polyphenols include catechins from green tea, anthocyanins from dark berries, bioflavonoids from citrus, carotenoids such as lycopene and lutein from tomatoes, and resveratrol from red wine. These compounds optimize antioxidant protection in the skin.

Blueberries are packed full of natural polyphenols called *anthocyanins* that are responsible for their deep color. Studies have revealed that these anthocyanins naturally prevent glycation by stabilizing the collagen matrix in the skin and promoting collagen biosynthesis and circulation. Blueberries have also been shown to reduce the production of collagen-breakdown enzymes called *matrix metalloproteinases* (MMPs) and therefore halt the breakdown of collagen.

For many, the North American diet consists of over-processed and salty foods with low nutritional content, directly affecting blood pressure levels. Some studies have shown that individuals with high blood pressure have significantly lower skin capillary density, and hence worse skin, than those with normal blood pressure.

There is also a positive connection between skin health and gut health. Friendly bacteria known as probiotics that reside in the gut, such as lactobacillus and bifidobacteria are well documented as effective for treating certain infections, promoting a strong immune system and reducing skin inflammation. Oral probiotics have been shown *in vivo* to rebalance healthy skin microflora, optimize skin barrier functions, and boost cellular antioxidant capacity.

Probiotics also help to counteract toxic byproducts from the environment and/or poor lifestyle choices. They help to defend the lining of the intestine and increase the bioavailability and absorption of many essential nutrients. Common vitamin and mineral deficiencies can impact healthy skin, hair and nails, and collagen production. If you think you might be suffering from a deficiency, the most common ones to address are: Vitamin C, iron, calcium, adequate protein, biotin and other B vitamins, choline, orthosilicic acid, zinc, omega-3s and vitamin E. Talk to your MD or ND.

## Key Supplements for Healthier Skin, Hair and Nails

Collagen Support – **BioSil™**
As mentioned above, collagen is a key element for healthy skin, hair and nails. Studies have shown that a highly bioavailable and effective nutrient complex (choline-stabilized orthosilicic acid – **BioSil™** reduces wrinkles, improves skin elasticity, thickens and strengthens hair, and reduces brittleness of nails.

*Dosage: 1 capsule twice daily or 5 drops twice daily*

<u>Vitamin C and Lysine</u> – **Medi–C Plus**™
Vitamin C is an essential component for the body's production of collagen and a potent antioxidant that can help rejuvenate aged and sun-damaged skin. Collagen is also dependent on the essential amino acid lysine. Sufficient lysine will also prevent connective tissue and collagen break down.

*Dosage: 1 scoop daily mixed in water*

***2000 mg of Vitamin C and 1300 mg of lysine is found in 1 scoop of* **Medi-C Plus** *™.*

<u>Omega-3 Fatty Acids</u>
Essential fatty acids, specifically omega-3s in the form of flaxseed or uncontaminated fish oil, decrease the formation of PGE2 – a messenger molecule that promotes inflammatory pathways in the body. By decreasing inflammation, the overall stress on the body is reduced, thus helping to support collagen production and beautiful skin, hair and nails.

*Dosage: take up to 2 tbsp. of flax oil daily and/or up to 3000 mg fish oil daily with at least 1000 mg of EPA and 400 mg DHA*

<u>GLA – Gamma-linoleic acid</u>
GLA in the form of evening primrose oil, black currant oil or borage oil offers a wide range of benefits, from reducing inflammation to promoting the healthy growth of skin, hair and nails. GLA can also be effective for arthritis, diabetic neuropathy, menopause, eczema and other skin conditions, as well as cystic and painful breasts.

*Dosage: up to 3000 mg daily*

B vitamins
Vitamin B2, B5 and B12 are all essential for healthy skin and promoting skin growth, as well as strong hair and nails.

*Dosage: at least 50 mg of all B vitamins daily, taken with food*

Biotin
Biotin is a B vitamin that is vital for hair and nail health. Biotin helps to fight nail brittleness and promotes hair growth.

*Dosage: 1000-5000 mcg daily with food*

Antioxidants – Vitamin A (beta carotene) and Vitamin E
As discussed above, vitamin A is an antioxidant crucial for healthy skin that renews skin cells and helps to reduce free radicals in the body. Vitamin E aids the body and skin in healing after damage and is wonderful for preventing scars. Vitamin E also facilitates healthy circulation, enabling more oxygen and nutrients to the skin layers.

*Dosage: 400-800 IU daily of Vitamin E (mixed tocopherols) and a minimum of 5000 IU daily of beta-carotene*

Zinc
This mineral helps to build, repair and protect cells, thus playing an important role in cell renewal. Also plays a role in vision, hearing, sexual development, and immune function. A deficiency in zinc can lead to poor wound healing, weak nails and hair loss.

*Dosage: 15-30 mg daily with food*

## Iron

Symptoms of low iron include hair loss, pale skin, brittle nails, fatigue, and low immunity. Rule out an iron deficiency by testing ferritin (iron stores) with your MD or ND. Ferritin levels should be at least 50-60.

*Dosage: depending on the severity of the iron deficiency, 25-100 mg daily with food, taken with vitamin C for optimal absorption. Choose highly bioavailable forms of iron such as iron bisglycinate, citrate or ferric pyrophosphate.*

## Probiotics

A healthy digestive tract is important to prevent the accumulation of harmful and "bad" bacteria. Having adequate "good" bacteria helps the digestive system remove any harmful toxins through the bowels and ensures optimal vitamin and mineral absorption.

*Dosage: at least 10-20 billion CFUs per day with meals*

## Hyaluronic Acid (HA)

Hyaluronic acid is a naturally occurring polysaccharide (carbohydrate) in the human body that helps to hold in moisture and firmness, aiding in tissue repair and holding together the skin's structural components (collagen and elastin). Hyaluronic acid diminishes with aging and environmental stress.

*Dosage: 100-200 mg daily*

## EstroSense®

Healthy liver detoxification is essential for beautiful skin and collagen production, to ensure the elimination of free radicals and environmental toxins.

*Dosage: 3 capsules daily with food*

## AdrenaSense®

It is absolutely critical to support and nourish the adrenal glands to reduce stress. Chronic stress and high cortisol destroys collagen and thus leads to aging skin, hair and nails.

*Dosage: 1-3 capsules daily with food*

## ThyroSense®

Thinning hair, dry skin and brittle nails are all major symptoms of low thyroid function. Proper thyroid testing and signs and symptoms should be evaluated to rule out hypothyroidism.

*Dosage: 2- 4 capsules daily with breakfast and lunch*

*\*\*ThyroSense® can be taken with low thyroid medications such as Synthroid (at least 2-4 hours before or after taking this medication)*

CHAPTER **THREE**

# Collagen and Bones

Osteoporosis is a progressive bone disease that involves the slow degradation of bone mass and integrity. Osteoporosis comes from the Greek word meaning "porous bone," and is characterized by diminished bone strength, which leads to an increased risk of fracture. Osteoporosis is often considered a "silent disease" because it develops slowly over many decades and usually without symptoms, until unexpectedly severe backache or hip fracture occurs.

Osteoporosis is the most common bone disease in humans, currently affecting more than 200 million people worldwide. Postmenopausal women are most at risk, and the risks increase with age.

The biggest outcome of osteoporosis is bone fractures. It is estimated that osteoporosis causes approximately 1.5 million fractures every year. Of these, 250,000 are fractures of the hip.

If we look at the progression of bone growth throughout our lifetime, we find that bones grow steadily in length and density until our late teens. After this time, bones continue to increase in density but at a slower rate. Then, when you reach your 20s, bones achieve what is called "peak mass": they stop building density and natural bone loss begins.

After achieving a peak bone mass around age 28, women slowly lose an average of 0.4% of bone mass in the femoral neck each year. After menopause and with the loss of estrogen, the rate of loss is much faster. An average of 2% of bone mass is lost in the first five to ten years post-menopause. The rate of bone loss returns to 1% per year ten years after menopause.

## Bone is Living Tissue

Bone is dynamic living and growing tissue that is constantly being remodeled.

Bone metabolism involves the removal of old bone from the skeletal system (bone resorption) and the addition of new bone (bone formation). This process controls the healing and remodeling of bone during growth and following injuries such as fractures and micro-damage, which can occur during normal activity.

In the first year of life, almost 100% of bone is replaced. In adults, remodeling proceeds at a rate of about 10% per year. The cells responsible for creating new bone are called osteoblasts, and osteoclasts are the cells that break bone down. The structure of bone requires a close relationship between these two cells, and depends on their cooperation.

Adequate levels of calcium and other minerals, collagen production, and complex signaling pathways help to achieve proper rates of growth and quality of the bone matrix. These signaling pathways include the action of several hormones, including the parathyroid hormone (PTH), vitamin D, growth hormone, steroid hormones and calcitonin.

## The Missing Link – Collagen

Bone strength depends not only on the quantity of bone tissue, but also on the quality. This is determined by the shape and architecture of bone, the turnover rate between osteoblasts and osteoclasts, mineral content, and collagen.

The bone matrix is a system that involves two parts: a mineral phase (calcium and other minerals) that provides the stiffness, and the collagen fibers that provide the toughness and ability to absorb energy. The mineral portion (mainly calcium) comprises 70% of the bone matrix, and collagen makes up 30%. This combination of collagen and calcium makes bone both flexible and strong, which in turn helps bone to withstand stress. Variations in collagen production or a deficiency in collagen can therefore affect the strength and mechanical properties of bone, and increase fracture risk.

Another important role collagen plays in the bone matrix is to serve as the framework to hold calcium into bone. Each collagen fiber acts as a "calcium-binding site," whereby the more collagen there is in the bone, the more places there are for calcium to be incorporated. The combination of more collagen and more calcium provides a stronger framework and more bone toughness to help withstand fractures.

## Collagen = Healthy Bones

More collagen = more bone "toughness" and more surface area for calcium to bind to (more "calcium binding sites"). This allows the bone more flexibility and the ability to bend without breaking.

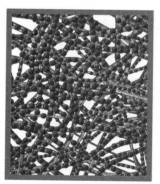 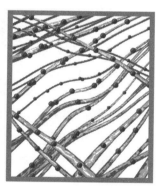

Less collagen = less bone "toughness" and less surface area for calcium to bind to, and therefore higher fracture risk.

## Risk Factors for Osteoporosis
- Family history of osteoporosis
- Gastric or small-bowel resection, celiac or Crohn's disease (low absorption and assimilation of calcium)
- Sedentary lifestyle

- Heavy alcohol and tobacco use
- Hyperparathyroidism
- Hyperthyroidism or excess thyroid hormone medication
- Postmenopausal
- Early menopause (physiological, surgical or drug-induced)
- Low calcium intake from diet
- Vitamin D deficiency
- Eating disorders (anorexia/bulimia)
- Long-term use of: corticosteroid therapy (prednisone or cortisone), chemotherapy or aromatase inhibitors to treat breast cancer, Depo-Provera injections, antidepressant medications called selective serotonin reuptake inhibitors (SSRIs), methotrexate, heparin, some anti-seizure medications, acid-blocking drugs called proton pump inhibitors, and aluminum-containing antacids
- Nulliparity (never having been pregnant)
- Short stature and small bones
- Caucasian or Asian race
- High protein diet
- Excessive coffee or caffeinated beverages consumed daily
- Excessive soft drinks consumed daily
- Heavy metal toxicity
- Stress!

## Signs and Symptoms

As mentioned above, osteoporosis is referred to as a "silent disease" because there are often no symptoms until one fractures a bone. There are, however, some warning signs that may indicate decreased bone density to help prevent fractures and worsening of bone loss. These include:

- Compression or stress fractures
- Gum disease or tooth decay

- Premature graying of hair (50% gray by age 40)
- Arthritis
- Low back pain
- Leg cramps at night
- Poor nail growth or brittle nails
- Decreased height
- Less skin elasticity and firmness

## Tests and Diagnosis

Osteoporosis is best diagnosed using dual energy X-ray absorptiometry (DEXA) to measure bone mineral density (BMD). DEXA is considered the "gold standard" because it exposes a person to considerably less radiation than other X-ray procedures. In the DEXA scan, measurements of both the hip and lumbar spine are taken. A baseline at age 50 should be encouraged, with re-tests done every two to four years. If any of the above risk factors apply, especially tobacco use, chemotherapy for breast cancer, amenorrhea (no period), prolonged Depo-Provera injections, menopause before age 45 or a history of fractures, DEXA scans are recommended earlier.

## Limitations of Bone Mineral Density

Bone mineral density is a wonderful way to increase the awareness of early signs of bone loss and establish a diagnosis of osteoporosis. However, it is not a complete measure of bone health because it does not measure bone **quality**, only bone **quantity**.

A bone's resistance to fracture is heavily dependent on its flexibility or "toughness" (its ability to bend rather than break). Bone mineral density testing is more an indication of the hardness or "stiffness" of bone and does not measure bone toughness, which is heavily dependent on adequate collagen formation in bone.

Also, bone density is not the only risk factor than contributes to future fractures. In fact, osteoporosis accounts for only about

15-30% of all hip fractures in postmenopausal women. Another important risk factor for hip fractures is an increased risk of falling due to poor balance and lack of muscle strength.

## Bones Markers – A Better Predictor of Bone Health?

Measuring enzymes and proteins released during bone formation and degradation compounds produced during bone resorption can gauge bone health and how the disease (osteoporosis) has affected you. These "bone marker" tests are useful for monitoring bone loss and success (or failure) of treatment. Some of these tests include:

- Osteocalcin - a marker of bone formation
- Urinary N-telopeptide of type I collagen - a marker of bone resorption, or loss of bone.
- Vitamin D - this measures whether you have a deficiency of vitamin D, which is essential for your body's absorption of calcium.
- Serum P1NP (Procollagen Type 1 N-terminal Propeptide) - formed by osteoblasts. Reflects rate of collagen and bone formation.

## Collagen Loss in Skin and Bone Density

There seems to be a relationship between healthy skin and strong bones. The connection may be a type of protein called *type 1 collagen*, a building block of both skin and bone tissue that is lost with aging.

Researchers from Yale University School of Medicine found that "women who had tougher skin had better bones." The depth and number of facial wrinkles and skin firmness were compared to variations in bone density at the hip, spine and heel. The strongest association of the facial wrinkles with the bone was between the eyebrows, which was more predictive of lower bone density than others.

Professor Sam Shuster also made the connection and proposed the same hypothesis, regarding changes in skin collagen as we age being associated with a higher risk of osteoporosis and bone loss.

## Supporting Healthy Bones with Diet and Lifestyle

Something that many physicians do not address in regards to healthy bones is the digestive system's role in ensuring adequate stomach acid is produced for vitamin and mineral (especially calcium) absorption.

As we age, our stomach acid and absorption capability decrease, making us very vulnerable to vitamin and mineral deficiencies. In fact, decreased stomach acid is seen in as many as 40% of post-menopausal women. There is also an association between increased risk of hip fractures and long-term use of proton-pump-inhibiting, acid-blocking drugs (PPIs), such as Losec, Prevacid, Nexium, Pariet and Panteloc. These PPI drugs rank as the third highest selling drug class in the United States and work by drastically reducing the amount of acid produced by the stomach, which unfortunately leads to a reduction of vitamin and mineral absorption

When supplementing to increase calcium in the body and the bones, the form of calcium is critical. Avoid calcium carbonate, as it's the most difficult form to absorb. A common recommendation by many medical doctors is calcium in the form of the antacid medication TUMS. TUMS will actually slow down the absorption of calcium by blocking stomach acid and is therefore a very, very poor choice. Choose calcium citrate or malate instead. This is what calcium is called when purchasing in a health food store – calcium citrate will be listed on the label.

If you choose to supplement with calcium, it's also important to include magnesium at a 2:1 ratio of calcium to magnesium. Supplement with magnesium or eat foods rich in magnesium like kelp, millet, tofu, beet greens, Swiss chard, buckwheat, brown rice, walnuts and kidney beans.

Milk and dairy products are often promoted as good for bone and for preventing osteoporosis because of their high calcium content. However, the results from long-term studies may be surprising. These studies have shown conflicting results between milk consumption and strong, healthy bones. In other words, high calcium intake from drinking milk doesn't actually appear to lower a person's risk for osteoporosis.

For example, a large Harvard study of male health professionals and female nurses found that those individuals who drank one glass of milk (or less) per week were at no greater risk of breaking a hip or forearm than were those who drank two or more glasses per week. When researchers combined the data from the Harvard study with other large prospective studies, they still found no association between calcium and fracture risk. There was even the suggestion that calcium supplementation taken without Vitamin D might *increase* the risk of hip fractures.

An interesting trend exists around the globe with regards to calcium intake and fracture risk. Countries such as India, Japan, and Peru have an average daily calcium intake as low as 300 mg per day (less than a third of the U.S. recommendation for adults), and the incidence of fractures in those countries is quite low. Other factors may come into play as well – such as physical activity and amount of sunlight – but it is still indeed an interesting observation.

Another observation reported by many complementary health care practitioners is that their patients have allergies to casein, the milk protein. The chronic consumption of dairy can also cause intestinal inflammation, potentially leading to malabsorption and nutritional deficiencies that would negatively affect bone health.

Luckily, there are plenty of non-dairy, calcium rich foods, which include:

- Greens – kale, collard greens, spinach, Swiss chard and turnip greens
- Almonds

- Salmon and sardines
- Sesame seeds
- Navy beans
- Brazil nuts
- Seaweeds – kelp, nori and dulse
- Goat's milk
- Tempeh (fermented tofu)
  (choose organic whenever possible)

Studies have also shown that a diet high in animal protein may promote bone loss by causing calcium excretion through the urine. Certain animal protein such as red meat and pork can acidify the blood, causing calcium and other minerals to be leached from the bones to buffer the acidity in the body. While meat's certainly not all bad, healthy protein sources should be encouraged, including chicken, turkey, fish, legumes, organic soy products, nuts and seeds, and eggs. Organic, hormone and antibiotic-free lean animal meats should be eaten whenever possible.

Another offender in osteoporosis is the high phosphorus found in carbonated beverages such as soft drinks. Serum phosphates compete with calcium in the blood for cellular absorption.

Other nutritional factors that speed up calcium loss from the bones and contribute to osteoporosis include:

- High salt
- Refined sugars
- Refined grains
- Excess caffeine in coffee, black tea, and chocolate
- Excess alcohol
- Smoking
- Dehydration (not enough water)

When it comes to preventing osteoporosis, a regular exercise program is as important as a nutrient-dense diet and supplementation. Weight-bearing exercises stimulate osteoblasts (our bone builders) to deposit in stressed areas of the bone and increase the secretion of calcitonin, a thyroid hormone that inhibits osteoclasts (our bone breakers). An exercise program for bone building should include weight-bearing activities (jogging, walking, stair-climbing, hiking) for at least 30 to 45 minutes three to five days a week, and strength-training activities (weight-training, yoga or Pilates) at least three times weekly.

It's also important to rule out heavy metal toxicity. Cadmium and lead can be stored in bone and increase bone breakdown, promoting osteoporosis. The most accurate method of testing is through the urine, which can be done by a naturopathic doctor or complementary health care provider.

## Key Supplements – Why Calcium is Not Enough

During bone growth and the early phases of bone calcification, silicon has an essential role in the formation of the cross-links between collagen. Remember that bone is actually made up of 30% collagen! The collagen in bone also helps accumulate more calcium deposition through its calcium-binding site. Therefore, increasing collagen increases calcium and makes for strong bones.

A highly bioavailable and effective complex (choline-stabilized orthosilicic acid – **BioSil™**) showed impressive clinical results in a double-blind study in postmenopausal women with low bone density. Compared with a control group who received only calcium and vitamin D, the addition of **BioSil™** (6 mg of silicon and 120 mg of choline as ch-OSA per day) increased the collagen content of bone 15% and increased bone mineral density at the hip by 2% in the first year. This demonstrates that **BioSil™** helps to produce greater bone strength and flexibility, thereby increasing resistance to fractures. *Dosage: 1 capsule daily or mix 6 drops in water or juice daily*

# Restores Bone Collagen Formation
## First 6 Months and Second 6 Months

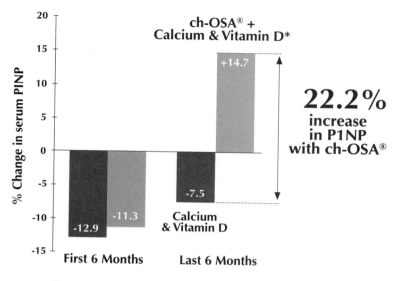

ch-OSA® +
Calcium & Vitamin D*

**22.2%**
increase
in P1NP
with ch-OSA®

*ch-OSA® (6mg/d); Calcium (1,000 mg/d); Vitamin D3 (800 IU/d)

# Improves Bone Mineral Density at Hip
## First 12 Months

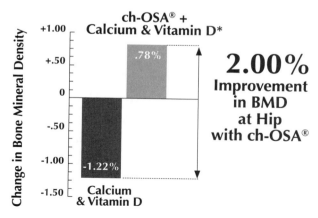

ch-OSA® +
Calcium & Vitamin D*

**2.00%**
Improvement
in BMD
at Hip
with ch-OSA®

*ch-OSA® (6drops/d); Calcium (1,000 mg/d); Vitamin D (800 IU/d)

## Calcium

Calcium is a key component for the prevention of osteoporosis as well as maintenance of good bone health. However, it must be remembered that calcium alone may only have a slight protective effect for bone health, and that a combination of the key bone builders discussed below is fundamental in any healthy bone program. The requirements for calcium increase as women age because of reduced intestinal calcium absorption, due to low stomach acid.

In the Women's Health Initiative (WHI) trial, hip fractures were significantly reduced in older women on calcium supplementation. The National Institute of Health (NIH) recommends the following:

| | |
|---|---|
| Premenopausal women aged 25-30 | 1000 mg/day |
| Postmenopausal women under 65 using estrogen therapy | 1000 mg/day |
| Postmenopausal women not using estrogen therapy | 1500 mg/day |
| All women aged 65 and older | 1500 mg/day |

There is a great deal of confusion and controversy about what form of calcium is the best. Oyster shell or bone meal calcium is often discouraged because of lead content. The most absorbable forms are often chelates that are bound to citrate, fumarate or malate. Calcium carbonate seems to be the least absorbable form.

***It is also important to outline dietary calcium before deciding on how much calcium is needed in supplement form.

**Check out the calcium content of foods that you are consuming on a daily basis before taking large amounts of calcium supplements. You may be getting enough from diet alone!**

*Dosage: 1000-1500 mg daily in divided doses.*

*\*\*\*Note: Calcium supplements should be taken at a different time during the day than thyroid supplements or thyroid medications and iron.*

<u>Magnesium</u>

When it comes to strong bones, magnesium supplementation may turn out to be as important as calcium supplementation. Magnesium regulates the parathyroid hormone and is necessary for the absorption of vitamin D. It's also involved in bone mineralization, with magnesium deficiency leading to the cessation of bone growth, decreased osteoblastic and osteoclastic activity, osteopenia (early bone loss) and bone fragility.

*Dosage: 500-750 mg daily of magnesium citrate, malate or bisglycinate*

<u>Vitamin D3</u>

Vitamin D is well known for its role in building strong bones and teeth, as it promotes calcium absorption and utilization in the body. Vitamin D deficiency is quite common among women with osteoporosis. Vitamin D has proven to be useful for the reduction of fractures and the maintenance of bone health. A meta-analysis of five double-blind trials (including a total of 9,292 individuals at least 60 years of age) found that supplementation with 700-800 IU/day of Vitamin D reduced the incidence of hip fractures by 26%.

*Dosage: 2000-4000 IU daily*

Zinc
Zinc is a mineral that plays an important role in bone formation by helping to form collagen in the bone matrix. It is required for the production of both osteoblasts and osteoclasts, and improves the actions of Vitamin D.

*Dosage: 15-30 mg daily*

Copper
Copper plays a role in the cross-linking and stabilization of collagen in the bone matrix and in osteoblastic activity.

*Dosage: 1-3 mg daily*

Vitamin C
Vitamin C is an important antioxidant that plays an important role in collagen formation, thus supporting the bone matrix. It also helps to reduce the risk of bone fractures in smokers.

*Dosage: 2000 mg daily or to bowel tolerance*

*\*\*\*2000 mg is also found in 1 scoop of **Medi-C Plus**™*

Ipriflavone
Ipriflavone is a synthetic flavonoid derived from the soy isoflavone, daidzein. It has been shown to slow down osteoclastic activity (bone breakdown) and increase bone-building activity. Research has found that treatment with ipriflavone for one to two years slowed bone loss in women during the first several years after the onset of menopause.

*Dosage: 200 mg three times daily*

*\*\*\*Note: although rare, some women develop low white blood cell count while taking ipriflavone, therefore have your white blood cell count and lymphocytes checked before and every six months while taking ipriflavone.*

\*\*\*All the above nutrients are found in **OsteoSense Plus** ™ in combination with iodine, quercetin, boswelia, turmeric and broccoli sprout powder. This is an excellent formula to help promote bone formation, increase the deposit of calcium into bone, promote proper absorption of calcium, and help decrease acute and chronic osteoporosis and osteoarthritis pain.

*Dosage: 2 capsules three times daily*

Vitamin K2

Vitamin K2 is important for the maintenance of healthy bone. It is required for the production of osteocalcin, a protein found in large amounts in bone. Osteocalcin attracts calcium to bone tissue, enabling calcium crystal formation to occur and thus supporting bone mineralization. Vitamin K2 is an important component of bone formation and remodeling. Many studies have found that vitamin K2 levels were significantly lower in those patients diagnosed with osteoporosis, and that decreased vitamin K2 intake was associated with an increased incidence in hip fractures in both men and women. MK7 (a specialized form of vitamin K2) has been found to be more potent, more bioavailable and have a longer-half life than MK4.

*Dosage: 100 mcg daily*

Boron

Boron has been found in research studies to reduce urinary excretion of calcium by 44%. It can also reduce urinary magnesium excretion and increase serum 17 beta-estradiol and testosterone levels.

*Dosage: 3 mg daily*

Folic acid
Folic acid and vitamins B12 and B6 help break down high levels of homocysteine in the body. High homocysteine is associated with cardiovascular disease and an increased incidence of osteoporotic fractures. This may be due to the fact that high homocysteine damages collagen, thus affecting the bone matrix and mineralization.

*Dosage: 400-800 mcg daily*

Vitamin B12
Vitamin B12 helps protect collagen from the damaging effects of high homocysteine in the body. Bone formation markers (osteoblast activity) such as alkaline phosphatase and osteocalcin are dependent on vitamin B12 status.

*Dosage: 1000 mcg daily*

Vitamin B6
Vitamin B6 also helps protect collagen from the damaging effects of high homocysteine in the body.

*Dosage: 50-100 mg daily*

Manganese
Manganese is required for bone mineralization and for the synthesis of connective tissue in cartilage and bone. Manganese stimulates

the production of mucopolysaccharides so that calcification can take place.

*Dosage: 15-30 mg daily*

Omega 3 Fatty Acids
Essential fatty acids in the form of organic flaxseed or uncontaminated fish oil block the formation of PGE2, a messenger molecule that promotes inflammatory pathways in the body. Increased inflammation is associated with disrupting the acid/alkaline balance in the body and the destruction of collagen. Elevated levels of PGE2 also correlate with increased urinary calcium excretion from the body. Reducing urinary calcium excretion would help prevent osteoporosis and reduce the formation of kidney stones. Essential fatty acids also help increase absorption of calcium in the body.

*Dosage: Take up to 2 tbsp. of flax oil daily and/or up to 3000 mg fish oil daily with a minimum of 800 mg EPA and 400 mg DHA.*

Probiotics – Lactobacillus acidophilus and Bifidobacterium spp.
Probiotics are known to have an important role in the maintenance of normal flora in the gastrointestinal tract. They are involved in the absorption and assimilation of important vitamins and minerals. A healthy digestive tract with adequate "good" bacteria will help maintain bone health by assimilation of crucial bone-building nutrients.

*Dosage: at least 10 billion CFUs daily with food*

## A Word on Bisphosphonates…

The most widely prescribed medications for osteoporosis are bisphosphonates. These drugs include Alendronate (Fosamax),

Risedronate (Actonel, Atelvia), Ibandronate (Boniva) and Zoledronic acid (Reclast, Zometa). Side effects include nausea, abdominal pain, difficulty swallowing and the risk of an inflamed esophagus or esophageal ulcers. That is why it is very important that those individuals taking oral bisphosphonates remain standing or seated upright for 45 to 60 minutes after taking the medication. Although rare, osteonecrosis of the jawbone can occur in some cases where a section of the jawbone dies and deteriorates.

These medications reduce osteoclastic activity (bone breakdown) and increase mineralization of old bone tissue, which, in some cases, will actually cause bones to become more brittle. In fact, although rare, atypical femur fractures are a concern with long-term bisphosphonate use and therefore these drugs are limited to five years at most.

## CHAPTER FOUR
# Collagen and Joints

### Joining the Body Together

We depend on our bones for support, but without mobility we would be nothing but statues! There are more than 400 joints, also known as articulations, in the human body that allow us to perform an array of movements such as throwing a ball, running, skiing, and even precise movements like threading a needle.

Bones work like the mechanical levers, and the joint between them is the fulcrum (or fixed point) on which they move. The strength and mobility of a joint is dependent on its ligaments, tendons and cartilage.

**Ligaments** are bands of tough, fibrous collagen and stretchy elastin that connect bones to one another. Ligaments are comprised of up to 90% collagen! They also surround joints to help strengthen and stabilize them, permitting movement only in certain directions. For example, ligaments are the most important stabilizers in the complex knee joint. Ligaments even support various organs including the liver, bladder, and uterus, as well as the female breast.

**Tendons** are rigid cords of tissue containing mostly collagen – about 80% of tendons are collagen! They secure muscles to bones and to other muscles, and are usually found in round or flat bundles. Tendons are covered by lubricated sheaths that allow them to glide easily without disturbing the tissue surrounding them. When a muscle contracts, it pulls on a tendon, which then tugs on the attached bone, and voila: the bone moves at the joint!

**Cartilage** is a dense, rubbery connective tissue composed of collagen fibers (about 70%), water, and a gel-like substance. It's essential to preventing wear and tear on joints. A layer of cartilage covers the ends of joint bones, cushioning them and reducing friction during movement. Cartilage also shapes various structures such as the ears, nose and intervertebral disks.

## Osteoarthritis (OA)

Arthritis is inflammation of the joints. Osteoarthritis (also known as degenerative joint disease) is the most common form of the 100-plus types of arthritis affecting more than 40 million Americans (80% of whom are over the age of 50).

In healthy joints, cartilage covers the ends of bones, reducing friction and absorbing shock. Osteoarthritis causes that cartilage to erode, and, as a result, affected bones grind directly against one another and cause accelerated wear. As the disease progresses, bone density decreases and osteophytes (bone spurs and cysts) may develop. These growths irritate surrounding soft tissues, often causing swelling and pain.

Osteoarthritis most often affects the joints of the knees, hips, lower spine and neck.

## Risk Factors

Factors that increase your risk of osteoarthritis include:
- Older age
- Genetic predisposition
- Fractures and mechanical damage
- Hormonal and sex factors
- Inflammation
- Obesity - carrying more body weight puts added stress on your weight-bearing joints, such as your knees.
- Other diseases - diabetes, low thyroid, gout or Paget's disease can increase your risk of developing osteoarthritis.

## Signs and Symptoms

OA will usually cause the affected joints to become stiff in the morning, but the stiffness generally only lasts about fifteen to twenty minutes. As the day progresses and joints are used, the pain and discomfort can get worse. Resting the joints tends to provide relief, but the joint may become inflamed with pain, warmth and swelling. The pain and stiffness causes the joints to be used less often, and the muscles surrounding the joint weaken. Loss of flexibility and reduced range of motion can also occur.

As the cartilage wears down over time, the joints may slowly become bigger (boney) as the body tries to heal itself. With severe OA, the cartilage may wear away entirely and the bones may rub together ("bone-on-bone"). When this happens, the joints can become extremely painful.

## Tests and Diagnosis

During the physical exam, your doctor will closely examine your affected joint, checking for tenderness, swelling or redness. He or she will also check the joint's range of motion. Your doctor may also recommend imaging and lab tests.

## Imaging tests

Pictures of the affected joint can be obtained during imaging tests. Examples include:

- **X-rays** - Cartilage doesn't show up on X-ray images, but the loss of cartilage is revealed by a narrowing of the space between the bones in your joint. An X-ray may also show bone spurs around a joint. Many people have X-ray evidence of osteoarthritis before they experience any symptoms.
- **Magnetic resonance imaging (MRI)** - MRI uses radio waves and a strong magnetic field to produce detailed images of bone and soft tissues, including cartilage. This can be helpful in determining what exactly is causing your pain.

## Lab tests

Analyzing your blood or joint fluid can help pinpoint the diagnosis.

- **Blood tests** - Blood tests may help rule out other causes of joint pain, such as rheumatoid arthritis.
- **Joint fluid analysis** - Your doctor may use a needle to draw fluid out of the affected joint. Examining and testing the fluid from your joint can determine if there's inflammation and if your pain is caused by gout or an infection.

## Chronic Inflammation and Collagen Destruction

Inflammation is a normal process of the human body. It is the first response of the immune system to infection, injury or irritation from a foreign substance.

The most common type of inflammation that most of us are familiar with is acute, the kind you experience when you sprain your ankle or overuse your muscles with heavy lifting. The body usually responds with redness, pain, swelling and warmth in the area.

Inflammation may also be associated with flu-like symptoms such as fever, chills, fatigue, and aching in response to infection from a virus or bacteria like the common cold or flu. When our immune system is performing optimally, inflammation helps initiate the healing process. The inflammatory process in the body is facilitated by the release of inflammatory mediators including histamine, prostaglandins, cytokines such as c-reactive protein, and interleukin-6 (IL-6). These mediators cause redness, swelling, warmth and pain. The whole purpose of the inflammatory response is to remove debris, attack foreign invaders (bacteria), remove cellular waste and encourage the healing process.

Unfortunately, chronic inflammation as seen in osteoarthritis can lead to oxidative stress and free radicals that can destroy connective tissue and collagen. This creates long-term inflammatory disease, pain and degeneration of joints throughout the body.

In some diseases, however, the immune system triggers an inflammatory response when there are no foreign substances to fight off. These diseases are referred to as autoimmune diseases, in which the body's normally protective immune system causes damage to its own tissues, including collagen. These diseases include Lupus, Psoriasis, and Rheumatoid Arthritis (RA), to name a few.

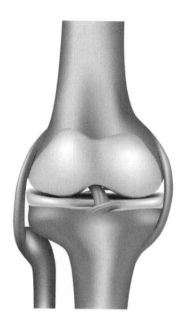 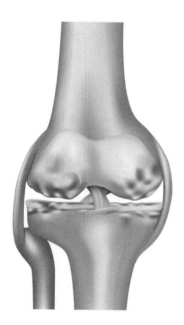

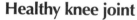

**Healthy knee joint**       **Osteoarthritis**

## Preserving Healthy Joints with Diet and Lifestyle

Dietary changes are absolutely essential for reducing pain and chronic inflammation. Research has shown that foods rich in anti-inflammatory omega-3 fatty acids, such as wild salmon and other cold water fish, freshly ground flaxseeds and walnuts may help to reduce inflammation. Increasing antioxidant-rich foods may also reduce tissue and collagen damage from chronic inflammation.

Always include a rainbow of fresh, local and preferably organic fruits and vegetables in your daily diet. Certain spices and herbs such as turmeric, ginger, rosemary and hops contain naturally occurring compounds that also combat inflammation.

## Common Foods that Cause Inflammation

There are some foods that actually CAUSE inflammation and destroy collagen. These should obviously be avoided, and include:

- Sugar - refined carbohydrates rapidly increase your blood sugar, which in turn causes your body to create large amounts of insulin. This will often result in a pro-inflammatory response.
- Red meat - too much red meat (aka eating red meat more than twice per week) will increase a pro-inflammatory fat called arachidonic acid. The human body needs some arachidonic acid, but too much can be toxic and can lead to chronic inflammation.
- Hydrogenated oils found in many processed foods - this one is pretty obvious! Pastries, convenience foods, trans fats, margarines and fried foods all promote inflammation.
- Dairy - dairy is considered a common food allergy that can put more stress on the immune system and increase the pro-inflammatory fat arachidonic acid.
- Gluten - again, a common food allergen that can result in an immediate inflammatory response for many when it enters the body.
- Too much coffee or alcohol!
- Some individuals will experience increased inflammation from members of the nightshade family such as tomatoes, potatoes, pepper and eggplant. For those individuals who are consuming any of the above in excess, reducing or eliminating these foods may be considered.

## Key Supplements

Collagen Support – **BioSil**™

Healthy joints are comprised of collagen-rich ligaments, tendons and cartilage. Chronic inflammation results in the degradation of these important structures, and thus results in osteoarthritis, weakness and painful joints. A highly bioavailable and effective complex choline-stabilized orthosilicic acid – **BioSil**™) helps to generate and preserve healthy collagen by stimulating our own collagen producing cells (fibroblasts). **BioSil**™ also helps to promote proline, an important building block for collagen and healthy joints.

## New Research

A brand new knee joint study on the complex ch-OSA found in **BioSil**™ has been announced.

166 people with painful knee osteoarthritis participated in a double-blind, multi-center, randomized, placebo-controlled study. Participants scored a grade II or III, documented by the Kellgren-Lawrence grading scale for osteoarthritis (see below), and reported a pain score of moderate or moderately severe on a 5-point Likert scale.

The Kellgren-Laurence Grading Scale is as follows:

Grade I: doubtful narrowing of joint space and possible osteophytic lipping

Grade II: definite osteophytes, definite narrowing of joint space

Grade III: moderate multiple osteophytes, definite narrowing of joints space, some sclerosis and possible deformity of bone contour
Grade IV: large osteophytes, marked narrowing of joint space, severe sclerosis and definite deformity of bone contour

Participants took 10 mg of ch-OSA (a.k.a. 2 capsules of **Bio-Sil™**) per day, morning and evening, and after twelve weeks of supplementation both the Western Ontario and McMaster Universities Arthritis Index (WOMAC) and cartilage degradation markers (CTX-II, COMP) were evaluated.

WOMAC results showed reduced pain and stiffness, as well as improved physical function in men taking ch-OSA (**BioSil™**), compared to men in the placebo group.

CTX-II stands for C-*terminal telopeptide type II collagen*. Type II collagen is the kind of collagen specifically found in cartilage. A higher level of CTX-II represents more cartilage degradation in the joint. These study results indicate that **BioSil™** decreased cartilage degradation and CTX-II.

COMP stands for *cartilage oligometric matrix protein*, and is a protein expressed primarily in cartilage, ligaments, and tendons. Higher levels of COMP are associated with cartilage damage, so it's a useful marker for joint destruction associated osteoarthritis, rheumatoid arthritis, joint trauma, and intense activity. As with the CTX-II testing, the ch-OSA group showed decreased COMP, which means taking **BioSil™** regularly for twelve weeks decreased cartilage degradation in the study's subjects.

*Dosage:* **BioSil™**: *one capsule twice daily or five drops twice daily*

## Vitamin C and Lysine – **Medi-C Plus™**

The Framingham Osteoarthritis Cohort Study concluded that a high intake of antioxidant nutrients, especially vitamin C, may reduce the risk of cartilage loss and disease progression with osteoarthritis. Vitamin C and lysine are key components for collagen synthesis and connective tissue repair.

*Dosage: Take at least 1000 mg daily*

\*\*\*2000 mg of vitamin C and 1300 mg of lysine are found in one scoop of **Medi-C Plus**™.

Curcumin *(Curcuma longa)*
Curcumin is the yellow pigment of the spice turmeric. Curcumin has a long history of use in Ayurvedic medicine as a treatment for inflammatory conditions such as osteoarthritis. The anti-inflammatory properties of Curcumin may be attributed to its ability to inhibit pro-inflammatory arachidonic acid, as well as neutrophil (a type of white blood cell) function during inflammation.

*Dosage: 300 mg one to three times daily*

Boswellia *(Boswellia serrata)*
Boswellia is a plant that yields a gum resin that has been used for centuries for arthritic and other conditions. Research shows that Boswellia has anti-inflammatory properties, and that it improves blood supply to joint tissues, lessening pain and swelling and increasing range of motion in the joints.

*Dosage: 400 mg three times daily*

Devil's Claw *(Harpagophytum procumbens)*
Extracts from the African plant Devil's Claw contain harpagosides – active compounds with potent anti-inflammatory, analgesic and anti-arthritic actions. Devil's claw has been shown to significantly reduce the pain and stiffness associated with arthritis.

*Dosage: 750 to 1000 mg three times daily (standardized to contain 2.5% harpagosides)*

Glucosamine, Chondroitin and MSM

Glucosamine is produced naturally in the body to help maintain and build healthy joint tissue that seems to break down with the aging process. Chondroitin sulfate is vital to the structure and function of cartilage, as it provides it with shock absorption properties. MSM holds our basic connective tissues together, forming the elemental structure of proteins, and also possesses a powerful anti-inflammatory effect.

*Daily Dosage: 1500 mg of glucosamine sulfate; 1200 mg of chondroitin sulfate and 1000- 4000 mg of MSM*

Omega 3 Fatty Acids

Essential fatty acids, specifically omega-3s in the form of flaxseed or uncontaminated fish oil, decrease the formation of PGE2 – a messenger molecule that promotes inflammatory pathways in the body. By decreasing inflammation, the overall stress on the body is reduced, thus helping to support healthy joints and collagen production. Omegas-3s also help support healthy cardiovascular and nervous systems, as well as beautiful looking skin!

*Dosage: Take up to 2 tbsp. of flax oil daily and/or up to 3000 mg fish oil daily with at least 1.2 grams of EPA and 400 mg DHA.*

## Serrapeptase

Proteolytic enzymes refer to the various enzymes that digest protein. *Serratia peptidase* (also known as serrapeptase) is an enzyme derived from silk worms that may be beneficial in inflammatory conditions. This enzyme helps the body break down immune and inflammatory complexes that cause many chronic inflammatory diseases.

*Dosage: 90,000 - 120,000 IU 1-2 times daily between meals*

## Hyaluronic Acid (HA)

HA provides a structural framework in joints and affects the ability of the cartilage to hold water. By the time most people have reached the age of 70, HA content has dropped by 80%, predisposing them to a decrease in connective tissue integrity, especially in the skin and joints.

*Dosage: 100-200 mg daily*

## AdrenaSense®

Supporting healthy adrenal gland function and the stress response is key in all inflammatory diseases, including osteoarthritis and autoimmune diseases.

*Dosage: One to three capsules daily*

## Celadrin

Celadrin works similarly to the essential fatty acids, EPA and DHA from fish oil. It is a complex blend of esterified fatty acids, which provides relief from pain and inflammation, improves flexibility, enhances mobility and lubricates cell membranes.

*Dosage: One or two soft gels three times daily*

## Vitamin D3

Several studies have shown that low serum levels of vitamin D appear to be associated with an increased risk for progression of osteoarthritis, especially in people under 60 years of age. Low serum levels of vitamin D also predict loss of cartilage, as assessed by loss of joint space and an increase in body growths.

*Dosage: 2000 to 4000 IU daily*

CHAPTER **FIVE**

# Collagen and the Cardiovascular System

The cardiovascular system is composed of the heart and blood vessels, and is responsible for delivering oxygen and vital nutrients to cells throughout the body. It also aids in the removal of cellular waste products. The Greek philosopher Aristotle influenced medicine for centuries by teaching that the heart was the body's most important organ and the seat of its "vital spirit."

Contracting and relaxing 100,000 times a day, pumping 2,500 to 5,000 gallons of blood through 60,000 miles of blood vessels, the heart keeps every cell oxygenated, fed, protected, and functioning.

## The Facts

- According to the World Health Organization (WHO), it is estimated that 30% of all deaths that occur around the globe each year are from cardiovascular disease (approximately 18 million people).
- Direct and indirect costs of cardiovascular diseases and stroke total more than $315.4 billion. That includes health expenditures and lost productivity.
- Someone in the U.S. dies from heart disease about once every 90 seconds.

## The Root Cause of Heart Disease: Inflammation

Inflammation is a normal bodily process that occurs in response to injury and infection. It is a part of the normal healing process and includes the migration of white blood cells to the site of injury, and the secretion of a variety of chemicals by the immune system.

Inflammation, however, becomes a problem when it becomes chronic.

Chronic inflammation is thought to play a role in many chronic diseases including anything that ends in "itis" (such as arthritis, colitis, bursitis, and tendinitis). There's also another type of inflammation that may not be as obvious. This "silent inflammation" can reflect an underlying low-grade stimulation of the inflammatory process with no outward signs of inflammation. Silent inflammation can be a major factor in the development of many diseases such as **heart disease**, diabetes, allergies, cancer and Alzheimer's disease.

New research published in the journal *JAMA Internal Medicine* showed that people who get 25% or more of their daily calories from added sugar almost triple their risk of dying of heart disease. Even those who have more moderate levels of sugar consumption, from 10 to 25% of their daily diet, still increase their cardiovascular risk by 30%.

Overall, Americans consume 15.5% of their calories from added sugars; in Canada, the figure is 10.7%. Sugar, hence, has become a major contributing factor in many diseases such as heart disease and chronic inflammation.

## Cholesterol Myths - Cholesterolphobia

Cholesterol has gotten a bad reputation over the years, and while it's true that too much of certain forms of cholesterol can cause major damage in the body, other forms are absolutely vital to our health and well-being.

Cholesterol is produced in the liver and is actually a steroid that forms the backbone for the body's adrenal and sex hormones. It's also a structural component of all cell membranes and is crucial in the exchange of nutrients and waste materials.

Cholesterol insulates our nerves: our central nervous system (brain, spinal cord and nerves) contain nearly one quarter of our body's cholesterol! In fact, one large study conducted by Dutch researchers found that those with chronically low cholesterol levels showed a consistently higher risk of having depressive symptoms. This may be because cholesterol affects the metabolism of serotonin, our mood-regulating and "happy" hormone.

Cholesterol is also required for the digestion of fat and is responsible for converting sunlight into vitamin D. So while it's gotten some negative press over the years, you can see that cholesterol is crucial to our body's well-being.

There are two types of cholesterol: low-density lipoprotein (LDL), or "bad" cholesterol, and high-density lipoprotein (HDL), the "good" cholesterol. When LDL levels get too high, plaque will slowly build up on the walls of blood vessels and narrow the arteries, putting more stress on the heart and causing it to work harder. If too much plaque accumulates, blood flow and oxygen to the heart is obstructed, causing chest pain. If a blood clot forms and blocks the artery, a heart attack may occur.

HDL (good cholesterol) removes LDL cholesterol, carrying it back to the liver and protecting against the hardening of the arteries. HDL also helps break down cholesterol into fatty acids that are essential for cell membrane integrity.

Elevations in cholesterol levels may also be the result of low thyroid function and therefore it is extremely important to rule out hypothyroidism in cases of high cholesterol levels.

So remember: cholesterol is not necessarily the bad guy. Evaluating all your risk factors and maintaining a healthy ratio of "good" cholesterol to "bad" cholesterol is the best preventative strategy!

## So What Really Causes Heart Disease?

The following list has a huge impact on elevating bad cholesterol, increasing inflammation and increasing the risk of developing heart disease:

- Processed junk foods full of trans/hydrogenated fats
- High sugar consumption
- Smoking
- Sedentary lifestyle
- Chronic stress
- Inflammation
- Heavy metal toxicity
- Trauma

## Healthy Blood Vessels Need Collagen

The entire circulatory system encompasses thousands of miles of blood vessels, reaching virtually every cell in every tissue in the body. Three types of blood vessels – arteries, veins, and capillaries – make up this intricate road map. Arteries carry blood away from the heart; capillaries are the tiniest pathways and carry blood into the tissues; and the veins take it back to the heart.

All blood vessels except for the smallest are made of three layers of tissue. The innermost layer, the *intima* or *endothelium*, consists of a layer of endothelial cells and molecules known as glycosaminoglycans (GAGs). These GAGs line the endothelial cells and protect them from damage. They also promote cellular repair.

The middle layer, the *media*, consists of elastic and muscular cells.

The outer layer, *adventitia* or *externa*, is made mainly of elastic and collagen fibers providing structural support and elasticity to the blood vessels, especially the arteries. Arterial stiffening has long been considered a major risk factor for cardiovascular disease, therefore keeping arteries soft, supple and flexible with ample collagen production is the best strategy for reducing the risk of heart disease.

## The Process of Atherosclerosis

*Atherosclerosis* (or arteriosclerotic vascular disease) is a condition where the arteries become narrowed and hardened due to an excessive build up of plaque around the artery wall. The disease disrupts the flow of blood around the body, posing serious cardiovascular complications.

There are many theories proposed by researchers regarding the cause of atherosclerosis. The most widely accepted is that the process of atherosclerosis begins as a response to injury to the cells lining the inside of the artery. The list above (*So What Really Causes Heart Disease?*) includes potential causes of chronic inflammation that can lead to insult and injury of the blood vessels' lining.

## Homocysteine – A Critical Marker for Heart Disease

Homocysteine is an amino acid and breakdown product of the conversion of methionine to cysteine. Elevated homocysteine levels can damage the lining of arteries and the brain as well as destroy collagen throughout the body. Individuals who are deficient in folic acid, vitamin B12, choline or vitamin B6 will have increased levels of homocysteine and are at higher risk of heart attack, stroke and developing peripheral vascular disease.

Elevations in homocysteine are found in approximately 20 to 40% of individuals with heart disease. Other contributing factors to high levels of homocysteine include stress, excess coffee and alcohol, excess red meat, and low consumption of fruits and vegetables.

## Testing

I'm often asked which blood tests are the best for evaluating or predicting one's risk for heart disease. Below is the most comprehensive list I have compiled.

Total Cholesterol Panel - including total, HDL and LDL, triglycerides and HDL/LDL ratios

Apolipoprotein B (apoB) - apoB is the primary apolipoprotein of the low-density lipoproteins (LDL or "bad" cholesterol), and is responsible for carrying cholesterol to the tissues. High levels of apoB can lead to plaque that cause vascular disease (artherosclerosis) and has been found to be a better predictor of heart disease that LDL.

Lipoprotein (a) – high Lp(a) is a strong risk factor for coronary artery disease, cerebrovascular disease, atherosclerosis, thrombosis and stroke. Lipoprotein (a) levels are only slightly affected by diet, exercise and other environmental factors, and commonly prescribed lipid-reducing drugs have little or no effect. High Lp(a) predicts risk of early atherosclerosis similar to LDL, but an advanced atherosclerosis Lp(a) is an independent risk factor, not dependent on LDL.

C Reactive Protein (CRP) - a general marker for infection and inflammation. Ask for the high-sensitivity CRP (hs-CRP).

Homocysteine - a common amino acid, homocysteine is related to early development of heart and blood vessel disease. In fact, it's considered an independent risk factor for heart disease. Even slightly elevated levels can significantly increase risk.

Lipoprotein Particle Testing - approximately 50% of people that suffer from heart attacks have "normal" cholesterol numbers. Advanced cholesterol testing is now offered by specialized labs, which accurately measure both the density and number of lipoprotein particles. This may be a more accurate assessment of cardiovascular risk.

<u>Adrenal Function</u> - a salivary cortisol or Koenisberg test to determine how well your body is coping with stress. A Naturopathic Doctor usually performs these tests.

<u>Pulse</u> - a pulse rate of more than 76 beats per minute is a higher risk for heart disease.

<u>Blood Pressure</u> - high blood pressure increases the risk of coronary artery disease. Keep a log of blood pressure readings at least every few months either at home (using a home blood pressure monitor) or at the drug store.

<u>Heavy Metal Testing</u> - heavy metal toxicity of lead, mercury, aluminum, and cadmium can increase inflammation and trauma to the blood vessels, contributing to atherosclerosis and plaque formation.

<u>Ferritin</u> - high levels of this storage form of iron can also be a marker for inflammation and predictor for heart disease.

<u>Fasting blood sugars, HbA1C and Insulin</u> - diabetes, metabolic syndrome and insulin resistance can all increase the risk of developing heart disease.

<u>Oxidata Test</u> - This test is usually performed by a Naturopathic Doctor and assesses free radical burden in the body, which can

lead to chronic inflammation and increased risk of cardiovascular disease.

## The Dynamic Duo – Vitamin C and Lysine

Two-time Nobel Prize winner, Linus Pauling, discovered a breakthrough in how we treat heart disease. He proposed that heart disease could be prevented or treated by taking vitamin C and lysine.

Pauling based this theory on a couple of findings: first, that plaque deposits are made up of a special form of cholesterol called lipoprotein (a) or Lp(a). Lp(a) is actually a special form of LDL ("bad") cholesterol that forms the plaques that obstruct arteries, and can be tested through the blood by your MD or ND.

He also found that plaque build-up only formed in areas of the artery exposed to the highest blood pressures, or areas that were constantly being stretched and bent – in other words, highly stressed and damaged areas. Lesions or "cracks" would form in the lining of the arterial wall from chronic stress and inflammation, and expose stands of the amino acid lysine (another important component of collagen) and initially attract Lp(a).

The combination of both Lp(a) and lysine would then build even larger deposits of plaque, which would eventually reduce the inner blood vessel and block blood flow.

Remember that vitamin C is a key player in the production of collagen throughout the body, especially for healthy blood vessels. Another important observation by Pauling was that cardiovascular disease does not occur in any of the animals that are able to manufacture their own vitamin C. We humans, as well as apes and guinea pigs, have lost the ability to produce our own vitamin C and therefore must get it through our diets or through supplementation. When vitamin C levels are reduced, collagen production drops and blood vessels become thinner, weaker and more prone to damage and plaque formation.

Pauling recommended the combination of vitamin C and the amino acids lysine and proline to help strengthen weak and damaged arteries, as well as help to remove existing plaque. Collagen is produced from lysine and proline, and the whole process is dependent on adequate vitamin C. By increasing levels of lysine in the blood, the Lp(a) molecules would bind with the excess free lysine, rather than contribute to the exposed lesions in the blood vessels. However, some doctors recommend only vitamin C and lysine, as proline can be produced by the body and vitamin C and lysine can't. In fact, **BioSil**™ activates the specific enzyme the body uses to make proline!

## Preserving a Healthy Cardiovascular System with Diet and Lifestyle

One of the biggest myths out there is the theory that a high-fat diet will cause high cholesterol and thus heart disease. To clarify, it's actually the TYPE of fat you eat that is more important than the amount. Excess hydrogenated or trans fats will promote abnormal cholesterol and increase inflammation, whereas good fats such as omega-3 fatty acids improve cholesterol levels and decrease inflammation.

Incorporating the following dietary and lifestyle practices will help to reduce inflammation, thus lowering the risk of cardiovascular disease:

**Foods** - Dark, leafy greens, berries, healthy fats, nuts and seeds, fish, and legumes are rich in flavonoids and antioxidants that help to reduce CRP, homocysteine and inflammation.

**Fiber** - Fiber helps bind cholesterol and other potential toxins, promoting better elimination of those toxins and preventing free radical damage to the arteries. Research has shown that when a high fiber diet is initiated, there is a reduction in a variety of cardiovascular risk factors such as hypertension, homocysteine and obesity. Excellent fiber sources include psyllium, ground flax seeds, hemp seeds, chia seeds, legumes, oat bran and fruits and vegetables. A minimum of 40 grams of fiber should be consumed daily.

**Minimize stress and get enough sleep** - The stress hormone cortisol can have detrimental effects on the body when released in large amounts during chronic stress. Practice stress management techniques such as yoga, deep breathing and meditation. Also, support your stress glands (the adrenal glands), with vitamins and herbs (read chapter 6, *Collagen and Stress*, for more information).

**Stay hydrated with plenty of water** - A minimum of one and a half to two liters should be consumed daily to help reduce cholesterol levels, improve alkalinity, remove toxins in the body, and help flush out excess sodium, thus improving blood pressure.

**Keep tabs on your blood pressure** - Do regular blood pressure checks at least every couple of months if you have had high blood pressure in the past, or once every six to eight months if your blood pressure is normal.

**Reduce your intake of table salt** - Packaged foods that contain high amounts of sodium can contribute to high blood pressure. Choose herbs and spices to season your meals or use Celtic sea salt in moderation.

**Eat more potassium-rich foods** - Carrot juice, grapefruit juice, banana, kiwi, potato, yam, squash and avocado are excellent sources of potassium.

**Exercise** - a minimum of 30 to 40 minutes, three times weekly, combining both aerobic and non-aerobic exercise should be encouraged. Achieve and maintain a healthy weight to reduce strain on your heart.

**Spices** - Turmeric, oregano, cinnamon, rosemary and ginger all possess anti-inflammatory properties.

### Avoid foods that encourage inflammation in the body:

- Sugar - refined carbohydrates rapidly increase your blood sugar, which in turn causes your body to create large amounts of insulin. This will often result in a pro-inflammatory response.
- Red meat - too much red meat (more than two servings per week) will increase a pro-inflammatory fat called arachidonic acid. The human body needs some arachidonic acid, but too much can be toxic and can lead to chronic inflammation.
- Hydrogenated oils found in many processed foods - this one is pretty obvious!
- Dairy - dairy is considered a common food allergy that can put excess stress on the immune system and increase the pro-inflammatory fat arachidonic acid.
- Gluten - again, a common food allergen that, when it enters the body, can result in an immediate inflammatory response for many.
- Too much coffee or alcohol!

## Key Supplements for the Cardiovascular System
Collagen Support – **BioSil**™

Heart disease and atherosclerosis prevention is highly dependent on healthy collagen in the blood vessels, to support flexibility and protect against insult. A highly bioavailable and effective complex called ch-OSA found in **BioSil™** activates enzymes that generate healthy collagen throughout the body, helping to keep blood vessels strong and flexible.

*Dosage: one capsule daily or six drops daily*

<u>Vitamin C and Lysine</u> – **Medi-C Plus™**
Vitamin C is a powerful antioxidant that helps protect the body from unstable molecules (free radicals) that eventually degenerate our healthy cells. As discussed above, the combination of vitamin C and lysine helps to reduce the formation of bad cholesterol and hardening of the arteries, and promotes healthy collagen, thus preventing heart disease.

*Dosage: one to three scoops of **Medi-C Plus™** daily, mixed in water*

<u>CoQ10</u>
The use of CoQ10 for cardiovascular disease prevention and treatment is impressive. CoQ10 increases energy production in the heart muscle cells. Supplementation will improve the force of contraction of the cardiac muscle, increase antioxidant activity within the cardiovascular system, lower blood pressure and improve heart muscle performance.

*Dosage: 100-300 mg daily*

*\*\*\*Statins (low cholesterol medications) and certain blood pressure medications will deplete CoQ10, so ensure that you are supplementing with CoQ10 when taking these medications.*

<u>Omega-3 Fatty Acids</u>
Essential fatty acids in the form of flaxseed or uncontaminated fish

oil decrease the formation of PGE2, which is a messenger molecule that promotes inflammatory pathways in the body. Increased inflammation is associated with an increase in damage to the arteries, thus promoting atherosclerosis and plaque formation. Fish oil also helps to lower triglyceride levels.

*Dosage: take up to 3000 mg fish oil daily with a minimum of 1000 EPA and 600 mg DHA*

## Sytrinol®

New research shows the value in supplementing with a combination of powerful natural antioxidants including polymethoxylated flavones (PMFs) and a range of palm (alpha, delta and gamma) tocotrienols (analogues of vitamin E) to help lower total cholesterol, LDL cholesterol and triglycerides, while boosting levels of the healthy HDL cholesterol.

**Sytrinol®** is also a powerful antioxidant with numerous heart health benefits, like the reduction of arterial plaque, improved glycemic control and reduced blood platelet aggregation.

Studies show that the combination of the above ingredients found in the proprietary product **Sytrinol®** works independently of diet. This is great news if you are just starting to evolve your diet toward a more heart-healthy way of eating!

*Dosage: one capsule daily*

## Plant Sterols – **ImmunoCare**™

Sterols interfere with the absorption of cholesterol, which is why they prove to be so beneficial in reducing high cholesterol and LDL levels. The National Institutes of Health (NIH) recommends the consumption of 1.3 grams of plant sterols daily to promote healthy cholesterol levels.

*Dosage: one capsule of **ImmunoCare**™ daily*

<u>Niacin</u>
Niacin has been a well-researched and established therapy in cardiovascular disease due to its ability to lower cholesterol, lower LDL and triglycerides, lower Lp(a) and increase HDL cholesterol. Side effects commonly occur with niacin and many individuals will discontinue therapy due to skin "flushing" and itching. Inositol hexaniacinate is the form of niacin that is well tolerated. It does not cause the "flushing" to any great extent, or the other side effects commonly associated with high doses of regular niacin.

*Dosage: 500 mg one to three times daily (inositol hexaniacinate), or begin at a lower dose of 100 mg two times daily (niacin) to avoid many of the above side effects often experienced with regular niacin, and increase gradually*

<u>Vitamin E – Mixed Tocopherols</u>
Vitamin E is known for its antioxidant, immune-enhancing, anti-inflammatory and anti-platelet aggregation effects. Many studies have shown its usefulness in the prevention of cardiovascular disease, cancer, cataracts and complications of diabetes.

*Dosage: 400-1000 IU daily*

*\*\*\*Note: do not take with prescription blood thinners such as Warfarin or Coumadin*

## Magnesium Bisglycinate - **MagSense**™

Magnesium is one of the most important vitamins for cardiovascular disease prevention and heart health. It is responsible for keeping the heart strong by supporting contraction, increasing HDL levels, and inhibiting platelet aggregation. Studies have shown that magnesium is beneficial for high blood pressure, arrhythmias, heart palpitations and many other heart conditions and symptoms.

*Dosage: 200-600 mg daily or one or two scoops of **MagSense**™ daily*

## Vitamin D

Most people suffering from atherosclerosis and heart disease are chronically deficient in vitamin D. There is a strong inverse relationship between vitamin D levels and artery calcification, i.e. the more vitamin D in the blood, the less calcification. Artery cells have vitamin D receptors (VDR) that, when stimulated by vitamin D, inhibit the deposit of calcium.

*Dosage: 2000-4000 IU daily*

## L-Arginine

L-arginine is an amino acid that is not only made in the body but is present in the diet as well. It is an important building block for protein synthesis and is a precursor to nitric oxide, which promotes vasodilation and relaxation of blood vessels. For this reason, L-arginine improves blood flow, reduces blood pressure and helps ease the pain from angina. L-arginine also supports the immune system and helps wound healing.

*Dosage: 1000–3000 mg daily*

## L-Carnitine

L-carnitine is an amino acid found naturally in the body. It is synthesized in the liver, kidney and brain from lysine by a process that requires vitamin C, iron, vitamin B6 and niacin. L-carnitine plays a key role in energy production and enhances fat metabolism, thus helping to reduce total and LDL cholesterol levels and triglycerides. Individuals who take L-carnitine have demonstrated lower levels of Lp(a).

*Dosage: 1000-3000 mg daily*

## Folic acid, B6, B12 and Choline

Homocysteine, as mentioned above, is a marker for heart disease and chronic inflammation in the body. With adequate vitamin B12, folic acid and vitamin B6, our bodies can recycle homocysteine back to methionine or change it to a helpful cysteine. Without sufficient B12, folic acid, and vitamin B6, however, homocysteine levels rise, leading to increased risk of coronary heart disease, stroke and peripheral vascular disease.

*Dosages: folic acid 400 mcg-3 mg daily, vitamin B12 400-1000 mcg daily and vitamin B6 25-100 mg daily, choline: up to 1000 mg daily*

## Hawthorn – *Crataegus oxyacantha*

The berries, leaves and flowers of Hawthorn have been used traditionally as cardiac tonics in a variety of heart disorders. The cardioprotective ingredient comes from its flavonoid content, specifically the proanthocyanidin, which gives the herb significant antioxidant activity. Hawthorn increases coronary blood flow, thus improving the utilization of oxygen by the heart. In addition, this herb is effective for hypertension, reducing cholesterol (LDL and triglycerides) and for preventing atherosclerosis and heart disease.

*Dosage: 100-250 mg daily (1.8% vitexin or 20% procyanidins)*

Garlic
Garlic is a popular lipid-lowering agent that has been reported to inhibit cholesterol synthesis. It improves circulation and reduces high blood pressure. Use liberally in foods or take as a supplement.

*Dosage: 1000-3000 mg daily*

Thyroid Support – **ThyroSense®**
Hypothyroidism is associated with elevated levels of cholesterol. Check thyroid hormones and supplement if TSH levels are above 2.0

*Dosage: 2 capsules twice daily with breakfast and lunch*

Adrenal Support – **AdrenaSense®**
Chronic stress promotes the release of cytokines, which are inflammatory molecules. Chronic inflammation can damage blood vessels and lead to atherosclerosis, thus increasing blood pressure and the risk of heart attack and coronary heart disease.

*Dosage: one capsule one to three times daily*

.

## CHAPTER SIX
# Collagen and Stress

Stress is a part of everyday life. It can affect the body physically, emotionally, mentally and spiritually. In essence, stress is multifaceted.

How an individual perceives and deals with that stress will determine their overall health and the impact that stress will have on the body.

## Facts

- Money, work and the economy continue to be the most frequently cited causes of stress for Americans, as they have every year for the past 5 years.
- 80% of all workers feel stress on the job – **that is 320 million Americans!**
- Job stress is estimated to cost U.S. industry more than **$300 billion a year** in absenteeism, turnover, diminished productivity and medical, legal and insurance costs.
- Unhealthy behaviors due to stress include: skipping meals, overeating or eating unhealthy foods, trouble sleeping and lying awake at night.
- Women report higher levels of stress than men.

Your adrenal glands are your stress glands and they control the most powerful hormones in the body, which affect virtually every system in the body. These glands are small, triangular-shaped glands that sit on top of each kidney. You cannot live without your adrenal glands and their hormones, and how well your adrenal glands function greatly influences your quality of life and vitality.

The hormones secreted by your adrenal glands have influence on all of the major physiological processes in the body: inflammation and collagen production; blood sugar regulation; cardiovascular and gastrointestinal functions; function of the immune system and nervous system; and hormonal health, to name a few.

Each adrenal gland is made of two parts – the outer region is called the *cortex* and the inner region is called the *medulla*.

The adrenal cortex secretes a variety of steroid hormones: glucocorticoids (cortisol), mineralocorticoids (aldosterone) and androgens (testosterone). The glucocorticoids have an effect on raising blood sugar levels. Mineralocorticoids have an effect on mineral metabolism and maintenance of healthy blood pressure. The adrenal cortex also secretes precursor hormones to androgens, such as testosterone and other steroid hormones (estrogen and progesterone).

The adrenal medulla consists of a group of hormones called *catecholamines* (epinephrine and norepinephrine, also known as adrenaline and noradrenaline). These hormones are released in response to physical or mental stress, known as our "fight or flight" response. During the fight or flight response the heart pumps harder, increasing blood pressure and heart rate, producing an increased demand for energy. This causes blood sugar levels rise, as well. Blood flows to the brain and lungs, and muscles and cardiac output are affected as the body prepares to protect itself from imminent danger.

The problem arises, however, when we have too much chronic stress, causing the *relaxation response* or *recovery phase* (where blood pressure, digestive function, heart rate, and hormonal levels return to their normal state) not to kick in: lives are too busy, expectations are too high, and bills need to be paid whether you have the money in the bank or not. This constant stress causes sustained cortisol output, which is linked heavily to collagen degradation, inflammation, fat accumulation, a compromised immune function, bone loss, and even heart disease. Yikes.

Over time, sustained high cortisol output can cause adrenal gland exhaustion. Adrenal exhaustion or adrenal fatigue stretches from mild to severe, and is often caused by some acute, severe stress or ongoing, chronic stress. The stressors can be varied, ranging from emotional, financial, psychological, environmental and infectious, or a combination of these over a period of time. Adrenal fatigue occurs when the adrenal glands are no longer able to adapt to the amount of stress encountered by the body.

## Do you Have Adrenal Fatigue?

One of the most common symptoms of adrenal fatigue observed in my clinical practice, and usually the first symptom to appear in general, is low energy. Initially some individuals with adrenal fatigue may appear quite normal but live with a feeling of always having to push themselves or use coffee and/or sugar to keep functioning during the day. The feeling of being overwhelmed, not coping well and sleep disturbances will often encompass the adrenally-fatigued individual. The following *Adrenal Stress Indicator* questionnaire is used in my practice with every patient in order to determine the status of adrenal gland health and function.

Let's see how you score. (See next page)

## ADRENAL STRESS INDICATOR

Write the number 1 beside symptoms you have had in the past; 2 beside symptoms that occur occasionally; 3 beside symptoms that occur often; or 4 beside symptoms that occur frequently.

- ( ) Blurred vision/spots in front of eyes
- ( ) Hormonal imbalances (i.e. thyroid problems)
- ( ) History of asthma/bronchitis
- ( ) Prolonged exposure to stress (job, family, illness, caregiving)
- ( ) Headaches
- ( ) Environmental or chemical exposure or sensitivities
- ( ) Hypoglycemia/blood sugar problems – Mood swings
- ( ) Food allergies
- ( ) Poor concentration/memory problems (Alzheimer's disease)
- ( ) Low energy, excessive fatigue
- ( ) Easily overwhelmed, inability to handle stress
- ( ) Post-exertion fatigue
- ( ) Dizziness upon standing (or fainting)
- ( ) Inflammatory conditions (Arthritis, bursitis)
- ( ) Nervousness/anxiety, depression, irritability or anger
- ( ) Shortness of breath/yawning (air hunger)
- ( ) Cold hands or feet
- ( ) Low back pain, knee problems, sore muscles
- ( ) Insomnia/frequent waking
- ( ) Excessive urination
- ( ) Excessive perspiration or no perspiration
- ( ) Heart palpitations
- ( ) Edema of extremities or general edema
- ( ) Eyes light-sensitive
- ( ) Cravings: sugar, salt or coffee and other stimulants
- ( ) Alcohol intolerance
- ( ) Recurrent colds or infections
- ( ) Digestive problems, ulcers
- ( ) Weight gain or weight loss
- ( ) High or low blood pressure
- ( ) **Total Score**

If you scored…

- Between 30 and 50, you've received an early warning that your adrenals are starting to weaken
- Between 50 and 80 – start with adrenal support such as **AdrenaSense®**
- Between 80 and 100 – your adrenal glands are taxed – you might want to take an adrenal glandular with your **AdrenaSense®**
- Over 100 – you are suffering from adrenal exhaustion and will require long-term adrenal support

Unfortunately, today most individuals who suffer from adrenal fatigue are often misdiagnosed by conventional medicine, even though the individual may exhibit all of the classic symptoms.

There are, however, tests in addition to the above questionnaire that are usually performed by naturopathic doctors or complementary health care providers, used to assess adrenal function. These tests include:

- **Saliva Adrenal Profile Testing** – Saliva hormone testing measures the amounts of various stress hormones in the saliva instead of blood or urine. Saliva testing measures the free (bioavailable) portion of hormones. This method is preferred for measuring adrenal health through testing levels of the adrenal hormone, cortisol. Saliva testing usually requires collection either in the am and pm (two point) or am, noon, evening and bedtime (four point).
- **Ragland Effect** – Postural Hypotension – Normally, when a person goes from the lying position to standing, the systolic blood pressure should elevate 5-10 mm Hg (millimeters of mercury). In adrenal fatigue, the systolic blood pressure from lying to standing will either drop or stay the same. The level of drop in blood pressure can help determine the level of adrenal fatigue.

- **Pupillary Response** – Adrenal fatigue will cause an imbalance between sodium and potassium. One of the signs of this electrolyte imbalance is the pupillary reflex. Normally, shining a light into a person's eye will cause the pupil to constrict and remain constricted for 30 seconds. In the adrenally-fatigued individual (especially in the later stages), the pupil will fluctuate between open and closed in response to the light, or the pupil will initially constrict but will dilate, even with continued light, in less than 30 seconds.

- **Koenisberg Test** – This is a urinary test that measures chloride and gives an indirect measurement of sodium and potassium excretion. Many Naturopathic Doctors use this test in their clinics.

In addition, I always thoroughly review patients' history, looking at all stressful events, including surgeries and hospitals stays; illnesses such as a bad bout of the flu, pneumonia, long term pain, dental work such as a root canal or implants; emotional stress such as job loss, moving, death of a friend or relative, divorce, financial problems; and other stressful events.

## Cortisol and Collagen – Does Stress Cause Wrinkles?

YES! Cortisol is a steroid hormone produced by the adrenal cortex of the adrenal glands. When produced in normal and healthy amounts, cortisol functions to reduce inflammation and helps the body adapt and cope with stress.

However, when released in response to repeated and prolonged stress, high levels of cortisol can have a detrimental and opposite effect on the body – creating more inflammation.

Stress studies conducted on laboratory rats have revealed that collagen loss in the skin is ten times greater than in any other tissue during chronic stress. It is one of the biggest culprits of dull, thin, and sagging skin. Remember that during stress the body prioritizes what is important for fight or flight. Preserving healthy, wrinkle-free and young-looking skin is typically not one of those priorities!

Chronically high cortisol output can also lead to a state of catabolism – the breakdown of proteins in order to generate energy. During chronic stress and adrenal fatigue the rebuilding process is overwhelmed by the amount of catabolic hormones, and therefore broken down muscles and collagen are not adequately replaced. This can lead to chronic pain syndromes, chronic fatigue and fibromyalgia.

## Preserving Healthy Adrenals with Diet and Lifestyle

Fighting adrenal fatigue can be exhausting! Often people find themselves reaching for quick, easy and tasty snacks such as cookies, candy, and soda, and making that mid-afternoon coffee shop run to help them push through the day.

Unfortunately, the energy we get from these foods is short-acting and often puts more stress on your adrenal glands long-term. Strategies to help you nourish healthy adrenals through diet include:

- Use fresh, local, preferably organic whole foods when preparing meals and snacks.
- Avoid preservatives, especially artificial sweeteners (aspartame, sucralose), colors and dyes, and added hormones.
- PROTEIN! Include healthy, lean protein with each meal and snack to help keep blood sugars balanced and stave off cravings for the junk food!
- Keep healthy snacks on hand, like nuts, seeds, hummus, fresh fruit, and veggies.
- If coffee is a must, try to limit it to one cup of organic coffee first thing in the morning, accompanied with a protein-rich and nutritious breakfast. Never substitute coffee for breakfast!

Your stress hormone cortisol follows your body's natural circadian rhythm. Cortisol levels typically rise around 6 am, peak around 8 am, and then throughout the day naturally rise and fall as needed. Levels tend to taper off at night and reach their lowest while we're sleeping. The timing and quality of our meals can determine healthy cortisol levels and affect its cycle in our body.

Eat to support your natural cortisol cycle and healthy adrenal glands with these guidelines:

- Eat a protein-rich breakfast within an hour of getting up, or by 8 am, to restore blood sugar levels that were depleted while you were sleeping.
- Eat a healthy snack around 10 am.
- Aim to eat lunch between noon and 1 pm to help stabilize midday cortisol levels.
- Make sure you eat a healthy snack (nuts, seeds, fruit topped with almond butter) around 3 pm to help offset that natural dip that occurs around 3 or 4 pm.
- Eat dinner earlier to help with better sleep, as your body can function better and concentrate on rest and winding down when it's spending less time digesting food. Try to eat dinner before 7pm.
- Eat a light snack one hour before bed, which can be helpful in regulating cortisol levels for a good night's sleep. Be sure to avoid refined sugars though! Nut butter with a small piece of fresh fruit is ideal.

## Key Supplements

### Rhodiola rosea

Rhodiola rosea has been studied extensively and has been categorized as an adaptogenic herb by Russian researchers for its ability to increase resistance in the body to a variety of chemical, biological and physical stressors. This anti-stress herb has a reputation for stimulating the nervous system, eliminating fatigue, enhancing work performance, and decreasing depression. Rhodiola also has anti-cancer and anti-aging properties, and may help with high altitude sickness.

*Dosage: 100-500 mg daily*

## Suma (Pfaffia paniculata)

Suma has been traditionally used in Brazil as an energy-enhancing and rejuvenating tonic, as well as a general cure-all for many disorders. It is excellent for the cardiovascular system, central nervous system, reproductive, digestive and immune systems.

*Dosage: 100 mg one to three times daily*

## Ashwagandha (Withania somnifera)

Ashwagandha is an important herb in Ayurvedic medicine. It serves as an adaptogen, helping the adrenal glands combat stress, and supports healthy thyroid function by supporting the synthesis of thyroid hormones.

*Dosage: 300-1000 mg daily*

## Siberian Ginseng (Eleutherococcus senticosus)

Siberian Ginseng has been studied extensively for its adaptogenic and anti-stress properties. Data indicates that it increases the ability to accommodate adverse physical conditions, improves mental performance, and enhances the quality of work under stressful conditions. Eleutherococcus has been studied extensively (more than 1,000 papers have been published over the last three decades on Eleutherococcus) and has a long and continued history of use in Siberia and China to increase the length and quality of life, prevent infection, improve memory and improve appetite.

*Dosage: 100 mg one to four times daily*

Schizandra berries *(Schizandra chinensis)*
Schizandra chinensis, a member of the magnoliaceae family, has an extensive history of medical use in China. This herb's adaptogenic properties increase resistance to a wide range of physical, chemical, and emotional stresses while promoting improved overall regulation of physiological processes. Experimental evidence suggests Schizandra has liver protective abilities and functions as a potent antioxidant.

*Dosage: 100 mg one to four times daily*

***All the above herbs are found in **AdrenaSense®**, an excellent product for supporting healthy adrenal function and combating symptoms of adrenal fatigue and stress.

*Dosage for **AdrenaSense®**: one to three capsules daily*

Collagen Support – **BioSil™**
A highly bioavailable and effective complex (choline-stabilized orthosilicic acid) is clinically proven to increase collagen production which can help offset stress-induced degradation of collagen throughout the body.

*Dosage: one capsule twice daily or five drops twice daily*

Omega-3 Fatty Acids
Essential fatty acids, specifically omega-3s in the form of flaxseed or uncontaminated fish oil, decrease the formation of PGE2 - a

messenger molecule that promotes inflammatory pathways in the body. By decreasing inflammation, the overall stress on the body is reduced, thus helping to support optimal adrenal function. Omega-3s also help support healthy cardiovascular and nervous systems as well as beautiful looking skin!

*Dosage: take up to two tbsp. of flax oil daily and/or up to 3000 mg fish oil daily with a minimum of 800 EPA and 400 mg DHA*

**B Vitamins**
Vitamin B6 – Pyridoxine and P5P
Vitamin B6 is a necessary cofactor for the formation of several important neurotransmitters such as GABA, serotonin, and dopamine, which are commonly associated with stress.

*Dosage: 100-250 mg daily*

Vitamin B5 (Pantothenic acid)
Vitamin B5 is an important B vitamin for supporting the adrenal cortex and regulating cortisol levels during periods of high stress.

*Dosage: 100-500 mg daily*

Vitamin B12 - Methylcobalamin
Stress often disrupts the body's natural circadian rhythmic secretion of cortisol. This disruption in cortisol levels can greatly interfere with melatonin production and lead to insomnia and other problems with sleep. Vitamin B12 is thought to help reset healthy secretion of cortisol during periods of stress, thus improving the stress response and quality of sleep.

*Dosage: 1000-5000 mcg daily*

Vitamin C

Vitamin C is very important because it's used in the formation of adrenal hormones such as cortisol. During times of stress, the body's requirement for vitamin C can increase ten to twenty fold.

*Dosage: one to three grams daily or to bowel tolerance*

*\*\*\*2000 mg is found in one scoop of **Medi-C Plus**™*

Magnesium Bisglycinate or **MagSense**™

Magnesium is important for the energy production of every cell in the body, and essential for adrenal gland recovery.

*Dosage: 200-800 mg daily or one scoop of **MagSense**™ daily*

*\*\*\*Note: some magnesium such as magnesium oxide or magnesium citrate can cause diarrhea even at low doses in some people, so reduce dosage to your own optimal level.*

GABA – Gamma-Aminobutyric Acid

GABA is a major neurotransmitter widely distributed throughout the central nervous system. Too much excitation can lead to irritability, restlessness, insomnia, seizures, and movement disorders. This must be balanced with inhibition. GABA is the most important inhibitory neurotransmitter in the brain and acts like a "break" during times of runaway stress and brain excitability. This supplement is ideal for those individuals who cannot "turn off" their brain.

*Dosage: 100-500 mg daily*

## 5-HTP – 5-Hydroxytryptophan

5-Hydroxytryptophan acts primarily by increasing CNS levels of serotonin, our "happy hormone." Serotonin levels greatly determine our mood, sleep and general well-being. Other neurotransmitters and CNS chemicals, such as melatonin, dopamine, norepinephrine, and beta-endorphin have also been shown to increase following oral administration of 5-HTP. During times of stress, the above neurotransmitters are depleted and therefore supplementation with 5-HTP may be beneficial.

*Dosage: 100-200 mg two to three times daily*

## Zinc

Zinc is an essential mineral for immune function and supporting healthy adrenal function.

*Dosage: 10-50 mg daily with food*

## L-Theanine

L-theanine is an amino acid extracted from green or black tea. In the brain, L-theanine increases dopamine, serotonin, and the inhibitory neurotransmitter glycine. Studies show that L-theanine can induce a perceived state of relaxation in an individual while staying alert.

*Dosage: 100-300 mg daily*

## Maca – *Lepidium meyeii*

Maca is a root vegetable cultivated in the Peruvian Andes that belongs to the brassica (mustard) family. Maca is rich in amino acids, iodine, iron, and magnesium. Maca increases energy and may be useful for supporting the body's stress response and healthy adrenal function.

*Dosage: two to four capsules daily of **Ultimate™ Maca Energy™**, one tsp daily of **MacaPunch Platinum Liquid Extract™** or one tbsp. of **Ultimate Maca Energy Powder™***

Probiotics – *Lactobacillus acidophilus and Bifidobacterium spp.*
Stress has a significant influence on intestinal microflora. Chronic stress will upset the balance between "good" bacteria and "bad" bacteria in the gut.

*Dosage: at least 10 billion CFUs daily with food*

## CHAPTER **SEVEN**
# Collagen and Menopause

Menopause represents a major transitional period in a woman's life. Most women enter menopause between the ages of 45 and 50. The term "menopause" is derived from meno (month, menses) plus *pausis* (pause, cessation), which is the true definition of menopause – one year with no menstrual cycle. Peri-menopause is the period immediately before menopause, which typically starts with changes in the menstrual cycle and ends twelve months after the final menstrual period. On average, 70-80% of women will experience mild to moderate symptoms, while 10-15% will suffer severe symptoms. These typically last between two and eight years, although some women may report experiencing symptoms for longer.

Common symptoms include:
- Hot flashes
- Night sweats
- Sleep disturbances
- Anxiety and depression
- Vaginal dryness
- Irregular periods
- Joint pain
- Brain fog and memory problems
- Fatigue
- Sore breasts
- Headaches
- Decreased libido

- Bladder incontinence
- Heart palpitations
- Weight gain
- Recurrent bladder or vaginal infections
- Increased risk of heart disease
- Increased risk of osteoporosis

## Early Menopause – More Common in Younger Women?

More than one in twenty women go through early menopause, which puts them at greater risk of heart disease, stroke, and osteoporosis later in life, according to researchers in a study of nearly 5000 women at Imperial College London. Women who had an early menopause were more than twice as likely to say they had a poor quality of life, "affecting vitality, physical function, mental health and general health perceptions."

Even some women in their late twenties and early thirties are experiencing early menopause, or what is often referred to as "premature ovarian failure." I have seen this too often after a woman has been on the birth control pill for years: she comes off only to never have her period restart naturally again.

Some of these younger women can even experience common menopausal symptoms such as hot flashes, vaginal dryness, decreased sex drive, bladder irritability, mood swings, irritability, anxiety and depression.

Why is this happening? Some theories have been proposed implicating environmental toxins, chronic stress, thyroid disease, smoking, trauma and a poor diet and lifestyle.

## Declining Hormones and Collagen

Menopause represents a natural phase in a women's life and a normal physiological process, but many doctors still see it as a disease.

In fact, in some parts of the world such as India and China, most women do not experience the symptoms Americans tend to associate with menopause. There seems to be a combination of dietary and environmental factors that play a role in this phenomenon. Also, in some cultures menopause is considered a very positive and celebrated event in a woman's life.

Many of the menopausal symptoms experienced by North American women are due to fluctuating hormones, namely estrogen, progesterone and testosterone. Declining levels of these hormones during menopause, especially estrogen, is accompanied by significant changes within the skin. Estrogens influence skin thickness, wrinkling, and moisture by binding to receptors on skin cells and activating skin cell renewal. Estrogen also helps to maintain healthy synthesis of collagen, and collagen atrophy is a major factor in skin aging: the loss of skin collagen in the first five years of menopause is 30%! Declining estrogen levels result in thinning of the epidermal and dermal layers of the skin, as well as a significant decrease in blood circulation and the ability for the skin to maintain strength and elasticity.

## The Missing Link – Supporting Healthy Adrenal Glands during Menopause

Juggling a career and taking care of family, finances and the house during menopause can become all too overwhelming, especially when our hormones are out of whack, too!

Adrenal fatigue is very common among the majority of people in our society, especially women. As women age and transition into peri-menopause and menopause, fluctuating hormones can put a lot of stress on the body. Keeping the adrenal glands well supported and strong before a woman reaches menopause can make this time much easier. On top of carrying the burden of stress, our adrenal glands or "stress glands" are also responsible for taking over hormone production when the ovaries shut down during menopause.

The adrenal glands truly are the foundation of hormone health.

## Lifestyle and Diet during Menopause

Nutrition and diet can greatly influence menopause and menopausal symptoms.

One of the most important dietary recommendations for all menopausal women may be to increase foods that are high in phytoestrogens. Phytoestrogens are plant versions of the human hormone estrogen. They're considered to be weak estrogenic compounds with an average of about two percent of the strength of estrogens. They can be beneficial when estrogen levels are either too high or too low. When metabolized, they bind on the same cellular sites as do estrogens, altering estrogenic effects.

The three main classes of phytoestrogens are isoflavones, lignans and coumestans.

Isoflavones are the most widely studied class of phytoestrogens, with genistein and daidzein providing most of the data. The best food sources of phytoestrogens are non-genetically engineered organic soybeans, flax seeds, oats, rye, lentils, fennel, chickpeas, alfalfa and sesame. Much research shows that women in Asia experience fewer menopausal symptoms because their diet contains a higher concentration of phytoestrogens, compared to women who adopt a North American diet.

There has been a lot of controversy recently about soy, and concerns about its safety. These concerns are based on its weak estrogenic and hormonal effects. Several studies have concluded that Asian women who consume a traditional low-fat, high-soy diet have a four to six fold lower risk of developing breast cancer. These dietary phytoestrogens have also been shown to inhibit cancer growth by competing with estradiol for the type II estrogen binding sites.

The type and frequency of soy consumed is also important.

My recommendation to patients is to choose organic, non-GMO forms of soy, as well as fermented soy products such as tempeh or miso. I recommend eating soy in moderation, meaning between 50 and 150 mg of isoflavones (phytoestrogens) daily.

For example, one cup of regular soymilk contains 30 mg and half a cup of tofu will contain 35 mg of isoflavones. Before making any conclusions about soy, it's important to remember that every woman is different and what may work for one woman may not for the other. Women with soy allergies may have difficulty digesting it.

Our North American diet is typically deficient in essential fatty acids (EFAs) which are very important in many health conditions, ranging from inflammation and PMS to menopausal symptoms. Supplementing with essential fatty acids from flax or, better yet, from a good quality fish oil rich in omega-3s will help with various menopausal symptoms. Also, a woman's risk of heart disease and stroke significantly increases after menopause, which is even more reason to include those healthy fats!

To reduce stress on the liver, enjoy foods plucked from the tree or fresh from the earth rather than packaged in a box or can. Spicy foods, sugar, hot foods and beverages and caffeine can trigger hot flashes, so keep intake of these items to a minimum. Dairy products and red meats have also been associated with an increase in hot flashes.

Cruciferous vegetables (broccoli, Brussels sprouts, cauliflower, cabbage and kale) contain indole-3-carbinol and sulforaphane, important nutrients for maintaining balanced hormones in the liver while reducing the risk of breast cancer. Ensure your diet is rich in these vegetables.

Boosting the amount of fiber in the diet is critical to preventing constipation and promoting the transport of harmful, excess estrogens from the body. Adequate fiber and healthy proteins help stabilize blood sugar and alleviate some hormone fluctuations.

Finally, new research shows that not only does a low Glycemic Index (GI) diet help to improve blood glucose levels, but it also helps people reduce food intake (possibly by making us feel full longer) and contributes to weight loss. Include low GI foods as part of a regular dietary plan.

## Key Supplements

Collagen Support - **BioSil™**

With the declining levels of estrogen during menopause resulting in the declining synthesis of collagen, supplementing with clinically proven ch-OSA found in **BioSil™** – will ensure healthy collagen production throughout the skin, hair, nails, bones, joints and heart.

*Dosage: one capsule twice daily or five drops twice daily*

Black Cohosh – *Cimicifuga racemosa*

Black cohosh has been used for a variety of women's health conditions, especially for the treatment of menopausal symptoms such as hot flashes and night sweats. Clinical and observational practice suggests black cohosh may be approximately 25 to 30% more effective than placebo for menopausal symptoms, including hot flashes. Studies have concluded black cohosh is non-toxic, non-mutagenic, non-carcinogenic and suitable for long-term treatment. Its use in Europe for more than 40 years in over 1.5 million cases demonstrates excellent tolerability and low risk of side effects.

*Dosage: 40-200 mg daily*

Chaste Tree Berry - *Vitex agnus castus*

The effect of chaste tree berry is on the hypothalamus/hypophysis axis. It increases the luteinizing hormone and has an effect of favoring progesterone production. Many women when transitioning into menopause will experience irregular periods, either too heavy or too frequent. Chaste tree berry is a beneficial herb to help normalize and regulate periods during peri-menopause. Women will also experience a sudden drop in progesterone when transitioning into menopause, which can cause mood swings, breast swelling, low libido and the above symptoms of irregular periods. Chaste tree berry may ease and prevent these symptoms during the hormonal shifts of menopause.

*Dosage: 80-160 mg daily*

<u>Dong Quai</u>
Dong Quai is known as the "female ginseng" and traditionally has been used for menstrual disorders, and as a supportive herb for menopausal complaints. Its effectiveness in relieving hot flashes may be due to a combination of its ability to stabilize blood vessels and its antispasmodic effects. It also contains ferulic acid which as has been shown to decrease hot flashes.

*Dosage: 100-200 mg daily*

<u>Hesperidin</u>
The flavonoid hesperidin, from citrus fruit, is known to improve vascular integrity and decrease capillary permeability, thereby strengthening blood vessel walls, reducing hot flashes and improving leg cramps.

*Dosage: 150-300 mg daily*

## Gamma-Oryzanol

Gamma-oryzanol is isolated from rice bran oil and contains a compound called ferulic acid that is responsible for its antioxidant properties. Ferulic acid may protect against various inflammatory conditions and has been shown to be effective in reducing menopausal hot flashes.

*Dosage: 150-300 mg daily*

*\*\*\*Note: All the above nutrients are found in* **MenoSense**®*, an excellent formula for the relief of menopausal symptoms such as hot flashes, night sweats, and insomnia.*

*Dosage: two capsules twice daily*

*\*\*\*Note: Can be used in conjunction with hormone replacement therapy (synthetic or bio-identical) and to help wean off of HRT.*

## Vitamin C

Vitamin C is a potent antioxidant that supports blood vessels, collagen formation, immunity, heart health and other health conditions. It may also help to decrease harmful PGE2 prostaglandins that increase inflammation and hot flashes in menopausal women.

*Dosage: 1000-2000 mg daily or to bowel tolerance*

*\*\*\*Note: 2000 mg of vitamin C is found in 1 scoop of* **Medi-C Plus**™*.*

## Vitamin E – Mixed Tocopherols

Research on vitamin E for the reduction of hot flashes, mood swings, palpitations, dizziness, anxiety and vaginal dryness suggests that supplementation may be beneficial. Studies as early as the 1940s found doses of 50-400 IU effective in decreasing hot flashes and other menopausal complaints over placebo. One study showed an increase in blood supply to the vaginal wall when taken for at least four weeks.

*Dosage: 400-800 IU daily orally, or insert vaginally, or apply topically to relieve vaginal dryness and improve lubrication*

## Vitamin B Complex

The B vitamins are important for liver detoxification and the metabolism of excess and harmful estrogens, and also help support the stress response and adrenal glands.

*Dosage: 50-100 mg daily*

## Calcium/Magnesium with Vitamin D

Calcium and magnesium both help improve relaxation and sleep. They maintain healthy bone density along with other bone builders, including vitamin K2 and D3, boron, ch-OSA, and manganese among others.

*Dosage: up to 1000 mg of calcium citrate/malate, 500-750 mg of magnesium citrate/bisglycinate and 2000-4000 IU of vitamin D*

## Omega-3 Fatty Acids

Essential fatty acids in the form of uncontaminated pure fish oil are very helpful in reducing pain, inflammation and hot flashes, and preventing heart disease.

*Dosage: 3000 mg fish oil daily with a minimum of 800 mg EPA and 400 mg DHA*

## St. John's Wort

St. John's Wort is one of the most widely researched herbs for the treatment of depression. Its mechanism of action seems to improve the activity of both serotonin and GABA, which help lift the mood and relax the brain and nervous system. Menopausal women often have major hormonal fluctuations that can deeply affect brain chemistry, thus causing depression, irritability, anger or anxiety.

*Dosage: 300 mg one to three times daily*

*\*\*\*Note: St. John's Wort may cause photosensitivity in some individuals; therefore, if you choose to supplement, be careful out in the sun. Also, it should not be taken with pharmaceutical anti-depressants such as SSRIs, or during chemotherapy.*

## Melatonin – **SleepSense®**

Melatonin helps to maintain the body's circadian rhythm, an internal 24-hour "clock" that plays a critical role in regulating when we fall asleep and when we wake up. Hormonal changes during menopause often put more stress on the adrenal glands and affect other hormones such as melatonin, which is another excellent reason why adrenal support is so important during menopause.

*Dosage: 3 mg tablets, one to three tablets dissolved under the tongue at least thirty minutes before bed*

## 5-HTP – **HappySense®**

5-HTP is another supplement that may benefit sleep as well as the mood fluctuations seen with anxiety and depression. 5-HTP is the precursor to serotonin, which is then converted into melatonin.

*Dosage: 50 or 100 mg, one to two caplets one to three times daily to a*

*MAXIMUM of 600 mg daily*

## GABA – Gamma-Aminobutyric Acid

GABA is a neurotransmitter that works like a "brake" during times of runaway stress. Stress excites the nervous system, causing irritability, restlessness, anxiety, insomnia and movement disorders. GABA helps to regulate brain excitability.

Dosage: 100-500 mg daily

## Maca

Maca has been used in Peru for thousands of years. It has proven to be useful for boosting energy levels, supporting the production of estrogen and testosterone, improving libido and providing relief of some menopausal symptoms. Maca seems to act on the hypothalamus and pituitary, two key players in hormone balance.

*Dosage: two to four capsules daily of **Ultimate Maca Energy**™, one tsp daily of **MacaPunch Platinum Liquid Extract**™ or one tbsp. of **Ultimate Maca Energy Powder**™*

## Adrenal Support – **AdrenaSense®**

Supporting the adrenal glands before and during menopause seems to be the missing link for most women. The adrenal glands are key players in menopause and take over the production of sex hormones when the ovaries shut down. Healthy adrenal gland function is therefore critically important to help women transition into menopause naturally and with more ease.

*Dosage: one to three capsules daily*

Thyroid Support – **ThyroSense®**

During menopause, the thyroid gland and hormones often become unstable, so thyroid gland support may be indicated. Some common low thyroid symptoms include difficulty losing weight, cold intolerance, fatigue and brittle hair and nails.

*Dosage: take two to four capsules daily with breakfast and lunch*

Liver Support – **EstroSense®**

Increasing liver detoxification is vitally important to the elimination of harmful estrogens and maintaining healthy hormone balance.

Important supplements such as milk thistle, turmeric, indole-3-carbinol, sulforaphane, calcium-d-glucarate, green tea extract, lycopene and rosemary extract help support estrogen metabolism through the liver and bind harmful by-products, thus promoting their elimination from the body.

*Dosage: two to four capsules daily*

CHAPTER **EIGHT**

# Environmental Toxicity and Collagen

Our environment is increasingly becoming more toxic each year, from the air we breathe, to the food we eat and the water we drink. All of us are living with some degree of environmental toxins in our bodies. For many of us, these toxins are causing us to be ill, contributing to chronic disease and heightened reliance on medical care.

These chemicals also create a very large toxic body burden and additional stress on our adrenal glands, immune system, hormonal pathways and detoxification organs such as the liver, kidneys and lymphatic system.

## Facts

- Each and **every second 310 Kg of toxic chemicals are released into our air**, land, and water by industrial facilities around the world.
- This amounts to approximately **10 million tons (over 21 billion pounds) of toxic chemicals** released into our environment by industries each year.
- Of these, over **2 million tons (over 4.5 billion pounds) per year are recognized carcinogens.**

## Chronic Disease is on the Rise

- Leukemia, brain cancer, and other childhood cancers have increased by more than 20% since 1975.
- Asthma prevalence approximately doubled between 1980 and 1995 and has stayed at an elevated rate.
- Difficulty in conceiving and maintaining a pregnancy affected 40% more women in 2002 than in 1982. The incidence of reported difficulty has almost doubled in younger women ages 18–25.
- Since the early 1990s, reported cases of autism spectrum disorder have increased tenfold.

The last 30 years of environmental health science shows that small amounts of chemicals can have long-term effects when the exposure comes at vulnerable times of development. Studies have linked early life exposure to chemicals to the later diagnosis of breast cancer, learning and developmental disabilities, and Alzheimer's disease. Research has linked chemicals found in building products, plastics, personal care products, and household cleaners to impairment of the reproductive system, increased risk of certain types of cancer, asthma, and developmental disabilities.

New research suggests that early life exposure to bisphenol A (BPA) found in plastics may be linked to an increased risk of the development of several types of behavior problems. The study published in *Environmental Research* (2013) measured prenatal exposure to BPA and found that this exposure was associated with internalizing behaviors, such as anxiety and depression in children.

Over the past decade, the Center for Disease Control and Prevention (CDC) has published data showing that exposure to chemicals like phthalates, bisphenol A (BPA), perfluorinated compounds, and cadmium are common.

The Environmental Working Group (EWG) is an American environmental organization that specializes in research and uses the power of information to protect public health and the environment. In 2005, EWG tested umbilical cord blood samples from ten babies born in US hospitals. Tests revealed a total of 287 chemicals in the group!

The umbilical cord blood of these ten children harbored pesticides, consumer product ingredients, and waste from burning coal, gasoline and garbage. Of the 287 chemicals detected in umbilical cord blood, 180 are known to cause cancer in humans or animals, 217 are toxic to the brain and nervous system, and 208 cause birth defects or abnormal development in animal tests.

The top five environmental toxins, many of which were found in the umbilical cord samples, are discussed below.

## Xenoestrogens – What are they?

Many of the chemicals that we will be discussing below are classified as synthetic xenoestrogens. The word xenoestrogen is derived from the Greek words meaning "foreign estrogen." Xenoestrogens are clinically significant because they can mimic the effects of natural, endogenous estrogen produced in the body. They do this by blocking or binding hormone receptors, which can be particularly detrimental to hormone-sensitive organs such as the uterus and the breast, as well as our immune and neurological systems.

Xenoestrogens can also alter estrogen and progesterone balance, because as they enter the body they can increase the total amount of estrogen, resulting in a condition known as "estrogen dominance."

Xenoestrogens are particularly resilient and stored in our fatty cells. The build up of xenoestrogens has been implicated in many conditions, including breast and prostate cancer, obesity, uterine fibroids, endometriosis, miscarriages, early onset puberty and menopause and diabetes.

## Top 5 Environmental Toxins and their Impact on our Health

The first step to reducing the load of toxic buildup in our body is awareness and avoidance.

### <u>Bisphenol A – BPA</u>

BPA is a very common chemical found in plastics, food and beverage can linings, thermal receipts and other consumer products. BPA is known to mimic estrogen, and studies have linked developmental exposure to BPA to reproductive harm, increased cancer susceptibility, and abnormalities in brain development and fat metabolism.

### Tips to Avoid BPA Exposure

Although completely eliminating exposure to bisphenol A (BPA) may not be possible, there are steps you can take to reduce your family's exposure to this chemical by avoiding common sources and limiting exposure for the highest risk groups.

- The developing fetus and baby are the most vulnerable to BPA. Replace plastic sippy cups with glass or stainless steel.
- Do not microwave or store food or drink in plastic.
- Almost all canned foods sold in the United States and Canada have a BPA epoxy liner that leaches BPA into the food. The highest concentrations are found in canned meats, pasta and soups. Eden Foods uses an alternative technology for their canned beans, but not their tomato-based products.
- Rinsing canned fruit or vegetables may reduce the amount of BPA you ingest.
- When possible, avoid polycarbonate, especially for children's food and drinks. This plastic may be marked with the recycling code #7 or the letters "PC." Plastics with the recycling labels #1, #2, and #4 on the bottom are better choices because they do not contain BPA.

- Avoid plastic reusable water bottles as well as metal food and beverage cans, including beer and soda cans, as epoxy resins (BPA) are often used to coat the lining of these consumer products.

## Dioxin

Dioxins are formed during waste burning, pulp and paper bleaching and pesticide manufacturing. They can disrupt the delicate balance of both male and female sex hormone signaling in the body. Recent research has shown that exposure to low levels of dioxin in the womb and early in life can both permanently affect sperm quality and lower the sperm count in men during their prime reproductive years. Dioxins are also very long-lived and thus can build up both in the body and in the food chain.

### Tips to Avoid Dioxin

More than 90% of human exposure to dioxin is through food, mainly meat and dairy products, fish and shellfish.

- Dioxins and other chemicals store in fatty tissue so try to eat less animal fat – buy lean meats and poultry.
- Purchase food products that have been grass fed. Farm animals are often fed food with animal products in it, which includes other animal's fat. This increases the amount of dioxin ingested by livestock and increases the amount of dioxin that is in the consumer meat product.
- Reduce your dairy consumption.

## Atrazine

Atrazine is a herbicide used to prevent weeds in crops such as corn and sugar cane and on turf, such as golf courses and residential lawns.

It is one of the most widely used herbicides in the US, and

was banned in the European Union in 2004 because of persistent groundwater contamination. As of 2001, Atrazine was the most commonly detected pesticide contaminating drinking water in the United States. Studies suggest that it is an endocrine disruptor and one study found that even exposure to low levels of atrazine turned male frogs into females that produced completely viable eggs! Atrazine has also been linked to breast tumors, delayed puberty and prostate inflammation in animals.

**Tips to Avoid Atrazine**
- Try to buy organic produce – check out the dirty dozen and the clean fifteen from www.ewg.org.
- Avoid tracking pesticides into the house by having everyone remove their shoes at the door.
- Vacuum carpets, mop floors, and damp-wipe dusty surfaces weekly, especially if you have small children who spend time on the floor.
- Filter your drinking water!

## Phthalates
Phthalates are commonly found in plastics to make them more flexible and as lubricants in cosmetics. There are many types of phthalates, among them DBP, DEP, DEHP, and DMP. You will find phthalates in perfume, hair spray, deodorant and anything fragranced, from shampoo to air fresheners and laundry detergent. They are also found in nail polish, carpeting, vinyl flooring, shower curtains and plastic toys.

Phthalates are known hormone disruptors and mimickers, which contribute to abnormal sexual development, obesity, and diabetes and thyroid irregularities.

**Tips to Avoid Phthalates**
- Avoid plastic food containers and plastic wrap made from PVC (recycling label #3).
- Some types of phthalates have now been banned from children's toys, bottles, etc., but these laws only took place in 2009, so avoid hand-me-down plastic toys.
- Stay away from fragrances. Instead, use products that are scented with only essential oils without synthetic fragrance.
- Find phthalate-free personal care products with EWG's Skin Deep Database: www.ewg.org/skindeep

## Perchlorate

Perchlorate is both a naturally occurring and man-made chemical used in the production of rocket fuel, missiles, fireworks, flares and explosives. Perchlorate contaminates a good portion of our produce, water and milk. It's a major health concern because it can disrupt the thyroid's ability to produce hormones needed for normal growth and development.

When perchlorate gets into the body it competes with the nutrient iodine, which is essential for the thyroid to manufacture thyroid hormones. The US Environmental Protection Agency (EPA) also states that perchlorate is considered a "likely human carcinogen."

**Tips to Avoid Perchlorate**
- Filter your water!
- Improve thyroid function by ensuring enough iodine in your diet.
- Try to buy organic as often as possible.

## What about Heavy Metals?

Toxic metals such as aluminum, arsenic, mercury, cadmium, and lead are often referred to as "heavy metals." These heavy metals from our environment are capable of accumulating in the body, especially in the brain, liver, kidneys, bone and immune system. Most of the heavy metals in the body are from industry contamination. In the Unites States alone, industries dump more than 600,000 tons of lead into the atmosphere, which we either inhale or ingest from our food or water.

Sources of heavy metal toxicity include:
- Aluminum - aluminum-containing antacids, aluminum cookware, drinking water, some commercial vitamins (Centrum).
- Arsenic - drinking water, rice.
- Cadmium - cigarette smoke, drinking water.
- Lead - car exhaust, dolomite, cosmetics, solder in tin cans, drinking water.
- Mercury - dental amalgams (mercury fillings), drinking water, fish and shellfish.

Some professions that are more susceptible to high exposure to some of the heavy metals listed above include battery makers, gasoline station attendants or airport workers, printers, roofers, solderers, dentists and jewelers.

Signs and symptoms of heavy metal toxicity are usually vague. Mild cases may be associated with fatigue, headache and "brain fog," or loss of concentration and clarity. More severe cases may involve chronic pain, tremors, anemia, dizziness, poor coordination and other neurological symptoms. Heavy metals have an especially strong affinity for body tissues composed of mostly fat, such as the brain, nerves and kidneys, and therefore can also be associated with high blood pressure and mood and brain function.

The best way to test for heavy metal toxicity seems to be with a challenge test. This involves taking a compound called a "chelator" that binds onto heavy metals that are hidden in the body tissues. The resulting chelating products are then excreted through the urine. The levels of heavy metals are then measured in the urine after the chelation challenge.

To help with heavy metals, avoid/minimize the above exposure and take the liver supportives discussed below.

## What is EMF?

EMF stands for Electromagnetic fields, which are a type of radiation that appear in the form of waves.

There are two types of electromagnetic energy – natural EMFs and artificial EMFs. The earth produces an electromagnetic field, and so does the human body. Natural EMFs are very low in intensity, and research shows that every cell in the human body may have its own EMF to help regulate important functions and keep us healthy.

Now, artificial EMF producers like hairdryers, cell phones, cordless phones, microwave ovens, baby monitors, GPS navigators and security systems create very powerful EMFs. These strong EMFs disrupt the body's natural energetic field. We are exposed to 100 million times greater artificial EMF radiation than our grandparents were, and that exposure grows each year.

Think about the stress all of these artificial EMFs put on the body, as well as our stress glands – the adrenal glands. They're just another challenge that the body must deal with and adapt to.

After an extensive review of 2000-plus studies, the National Institute of Environmental Health Sciences concluded that EMFs "should be regarded as possible carcinogens" and potentially very harmful and toxic to our health. In today's world it's virtually impossible to avoid all artificial EMFs, but we can definitely work on minimizing our exposure. Easy tips to avoid EMFs include:

- Minimize your talk time on cell phones and try to eliminate calls over 20 minutes.

- Don't wear your cell phone like a pager – if your phone is turned on and worn on your belt or carried in a pocket, you could be receiving a constant blast of radiation from the battery pack. Carry your cell phone in your purse or briefcase to minimize exposure.
- Minimize your time in front of the TV and computer.
- Don't use a microwave!

The book *A Wellness Guide for The Digital Age* by Kerry Crofton, PhD, is an excellent source of additional information as well as safer technology solutions for all things wired and wireless.

## Collagen and Free Radical Damage

Acting like armor, the skin is an effective defense system, keeping foreign invaders such as environmental toxins from penetrating it. The health and appearance of your skin is a key indicator of how healthy the inside of the body is. It can also be an indicator of collagen production elsewhere in the body, as a large portion of your skin is composed of collagen and dependent on it.

Skin aging and collagen destruction is influenced by many environmental factors, including our diet, ultraviolet radiation, tobacco use and environmental pollutants. As the outermost barrier, the skin is regularly exposed to UV radiation, air pollution and other environmental toxins. These exposures produce highly volatile molecules called free radicals, which go on to wreak havoc in the cellular environment of the skin, and destroy collagen. Chronic free radical assault often leads to unhealthy skin, giving rise to blotchy pigmentation, wrinkles and saggy skin.

Tobacco use is a major factor that contributes to many chronic diseases. On the molecular level, smoking produces oxidative stress and free radicals, increasing inflammation and destroying collagen throughout the body. New research from the Western Reserve University and University Hospitals of Cleveland, Ohio give insight into the cellular-level mechanisms by which smoking may lead to premature aging.

Researchers recruited 79 pairs of identical twins; one twin within each pair smoked, while the other had smoked for less than five years less, or did not smoke at all. Findings revealed that twins who smoked had significantly higher facial aging – more sagging of the upper eyelids and more bags on the lower eyelids and under the eyes. They also had higher scores for facial wrinkles, specifically wrinkling of the upper and lower cheek. Smoking can reduce the amount of oxygen to the skin, and was found to speed up the breakdown of collagen.

Chronic sun exposure also damages connective tissue and alters normal skin metabolism. In addition to depressing immunity and stimulating oxidative stress and inflammation, UV radiation increases the production of *matrix metalloproteinases* (MMPS), enzymes that degrade collagen.

The destruction of collagen is a major contributor to the loss of skin suppleness and structure that occurs with advancing age. UV radiation in the skin also results in the depletion of antioxidants such as vitamin E and vitamin C, which decrease the overall antioxidant capacity within the skin.

## Reducing Toxins through Diet and Lifestyle

To reduce the load of environmental toxins, the first step is to stop carrying toxins into our homes and into our bodies.

About 90% of our daily toxin intake comes from the air inside our homes and workplaces and the food that we eat. Some of us cannot make huge changes with the air quality at work, but we can definitely change the air in our homes. Using high quality air filters that are changed regularly (every six to eight weeks) is one of the best ways to reduce the toxin presence in your air at home. Opening the windows once a week when you are cleaning can bring in the fresh air and eliminate any accumulation of toxins. For those who are living in colder climates, bundle up and open the windows every few weeks and air out those pollutants and dust particles.

I also think one easy step that can be incorporated daily to avoid the buildup of household toxins is taking off your shoes! Many chemicals from outside (pesticides, heavy metals, etc.) are brought in on the soles of your shoes.

Another big source of toxin exposure as mentioned above is from the food we eat. I recommend to all my patients the Dirty Dozen and Clean Fifteen chart from www.ewg.org. This is an excellent guide for grocery shopping and outlines the fruits and vegetables with the highest pesticide residue, versus those with the lowest pesticide residue.

The 12 MOST TOXIC fruits and vegetables include:
- Apples
- Strawberries
- Grapes
- Celery
- Peaches
- Spinach
- Sweet bell peppers
- Nectarines - imported
- Cucumbers
- Cherry tomatoes
- Snap peas – imported
- Potatoes

The CLEAN 15 fruits and vegetables include:
- Avocadoes

- Sweet corn
- Pineapples
- Cabbage
- Sweet peas – frozen
- Onions
- Asparagus
- Mangoes
- Papayas
- Kiwi
- Eggplant
- Grapefruit
- Cantaloupe
- Cauliflower
- Sweet potatoes

Pesticide and antibiotic residues in conventionally raised beef, dairy products and farmed fish (Atlantic salmon) should be eliminated wherever possible. Organic and grass-fed beef and dairy products should be encouraged. Certain fish also contain higher levels of mercury content, like sharks, swordfish, king mackerel, tuna, marlin, halibut, snapper and lobster, and should be limited to once every six to eight weeks.

Fish with the lowest mercury content include: salmon, tilapia, sole, arctic char and clams. These types of seafood can be eaten two to three times per week.

## Key Supplements for Reducing Toxic Load on the Body
<u>Collagen Support – **BioSil**™</u>

As mentioned throughout this chapter, environmental toxins do have a significant impact on the function of our body as well as the production of healthy collagen. A highly bioavailable and clinically researched nutrient complex containing choline-stabilized orthosilicic acid – **BioSil™** – helps to generate and preserve healthy collagen using your own DNA.

*Dosage: one capsule twice daily and/or five drops twice daily*

Milk Thistle *(Silybum marianum)*
Research shows the most impressive support of liver function occurs in extract of milk thistle. Milk thistle contains a group of flavonoids that have a protective effect on the liver and also enhance detoxification. This powerful herb prevents damage to the liver by acting as an antioxidant, as well as preventing the depletion of glutathione. The antioxidant glutathione protects the liver from stress and assists in detoxification of harmful chemicals and toxins.

*Dosage: 400-600 mg daily*

Turmeric *(Curcuma longa)*
Turmeric is a well-researched herb that has shown to have potent antioxidant, liver protective, anti-inflammatory, and anti-carcinogenic properties.

*Dosage: up to 1500 mg daily*

**EstroSense®**
**EstroSense®** is a gentle and comprehensive liver detoxification formula to help with healthy estrogen metabolism, the elimination of harmful toxins, and prevention of toxic build up in the body.

*Dosage: two to three capsules daily with food*

*\*\*\*Note: Milk thistle and turmeric as well as powerful detoxification nutrients and antioxidants such as I3C, calcium-d-glucarate, sulfora-*

*phane, green tea extract, lycopene and rosemary extract are all found in* **EstroSense®**.

## AdrenaSense®

It is absolutely critical to support and nourish the adrenal glands to reduce stress, especially when dealing with the environmental insult that we are exposed to on a daily basis.

*Dosage: one to three capsules daily with food*

## Vitamin C

Vitamin C is a potent antioxidant and is required for the synthesis of glutathione, which helps support our antioxidant defenses while preventing free radical damage from environmental toxins and optimizing detoxification pathways. Vitamin C and lysine are important components of healthy collagen formation. Vitamin C may also decrease lead levels in the body, a toxic heavy metal.

*Dosage: 1000-2000 mg/day with food*

*\*\*\*Note: There is 2000 mg of vitamin C and 1300 mg of lysine in one scoop of* **Medi-C Plus™**.

## Probiotics

A healthy digestive tract is important to prevent the accumulation of harmful and "bad" bacteria. Having adequate "good" bacteria help the digestive system remove any harmful toxins through the bowels.

*Dosage: at least 10-20 billion CFUs/day with meals*

Fiber
Fiber in the form of psyllium, oat bran, chia seeds, hemp hearts, ground flax and fruits and veggies will bind onto chemicals and toxins and eliminate them safely through the bowels. Regular elimination (at least one to two bowel movements per day) is essential for reducing the toxic stress on the body.

*Dosage: at least 35-40 grams of fiber daily*

Lipotropic Agents
Choline, betaine, methionine, vitamin B12, folic acid and vitamin B6 are all important lipotropic agents that promote the flow of fat and bile to and from the liver. They have a decongesting effect on the liver and help optimize fat metabolism.

*Dosage: 1000 mg of choline and 1000 mg of methionine and/or cysteine daily*

N-acetyl cysteine - NAC
N-acetyl cysteine increases cellular levels of glutathione, a powerful antioxidant involved in protecting the body from environmental toxic damage. It has also been found to reduce toxicity and protect organs from the damage of lead, arsenic, mercury and cadmium.

*Dosage: at least 250 mg daily with food*

Alpha-Lipoic Acid
Alpha-lipoic acid also stimulates glutathione synthesis and has shown to protect against liver and nervous system damage from heavy metals and other environmental toxicity.

*Dosage: 200 - 400 mg daily with food.*

## Chlorella

Chlorella is a single-celled fresh water algae that is a potent detox agent for mercury and other heavy metals. Chlorella also has liver protective properties, is a potent antioxidant, and is immune-supportive.

*Dosage: up to three grams daily*

# References

Gaby, Alan R. *Nutritional Medicine.* Concord, NH. Fritz Perlberg Publishing. 2011.

Martini, Frederic H. et al. *Human Anatomy.* 3rd Edition. Upper Saddle River, NJ. Prentice-Hall Inc. 2000.

Murray, M. and Pizzorno J. *Encyclopedia of Natural Medicine.* Revised 3rd Edition. Rocklin, CA. Prima Publishing. 2012.

Pagana, KD and Pagana TJ. *Mosby's Manual of Diagnostic and Laboratory Tests.* 2nd Edition. St. Louis, Missouri. Mosby. 2002.
Passwater, Richard. *BioSil Presentations CHFA East/West 2013-2014.*

Silverthorn, D. *Human Physiology: An Integrated Approach.* 2nd Edition. Upper Saddle River, NJ. Prentice-Hall Inc. 2001.

## Chapter 1: Collagen – The Body's Building Block

*Altern Med Rev.* 2001 Oct;6(5):500-4.

Bellamy G, Bornstein P. Evidence for procollagen, a biosynthetic precursors of collagen. *Proc Natl Acad Sci.* 1971;68:1138-42.

Bienkowski RS, Baum BJ, Crystal RG. Fibroblasts degrade newly synthesized collagen within the cell before secretion. *Nature.* 1978;276:413-6.

Diegelmann, Robert F. From the Medical College of Virginia, Virginia Commonwealth University, Richmond, Virginia. *Wounds.* 2001;13(5).

Mussini E, Hutton JJ, Udenfriend S. Collagen proline hydroxylase in wound healing, granuloma formation, scurvy, and growth. *Science.* 1967;157:927-9.

Myllyla et al., "Ascorbate is Consumed Stoichiometrically in the Uncoupled Reactions Catalyzed by Prolyl-4-Hydroxylase and Lysyl Hydroxylase. *Journal of Biological Chemistry.* 1984;259:5403-5405.

Pauling, Linus. *How to Live Longer and Feel Better.* The University of Michigan. Avon. 1986.

Shoulders, M. D.; Raines, R. T. Collagen structure and stability" *Annu. Rev. Biochem.* 2002;78: 929–958.

## Chapter 2: Collagen and Skin, Hair and Nails

Antonios, Tarek F.T. et al. Rarefaction of Skin Capillaries in Borderline Essential *Hypertension* Suggests an Early Structural Abnormality. Hypertension. 1999;34:655-658

Barel, A. et al. Effect of Oral Intake of Choline-Stabilized Orthosilicic Acid on Skin, Nails and Hair in Women with Photodamaged Facial Skin. Archives of *Dermatological Research*, Volume 297, 2005.

Barel, A. et al. Effect of Oral Intake of Choline Stabilized Orthosilicic Acid on Skin, Nails and Hair in Women with Photodamaged Facial Skin. *Skin Research And Technology.* Volume 10, Number 4, November 2004.

Bouilly-Gauthier, D. et al. Clinical evidence of benefits of a dietary supplement containing probiotic and carotenoids on ultraviolet-induced skin damage. *British Journal of Dermatology.* Volume 163, Issue 3, 536-543 September 2010.

Gueniche, A. et al. Bifidobacterium longum lysate, a new ingredient for reactive skin. *Exp Dermatol.* 2010;Aug;19(8).

Gugliucci, A, Bendayan, M. Renal fate of circulating advanced glycated end products (AGE): evidence for reabsorption and catabolism of AGE-peptides by renal proximal tubular cells. *Diabetologia.* 1996;39 (2) 149–60.

Jeppesen PB, Hoy CE, Mortensen PB. Essential fatty acid deficiency in patients receiving home parenteral nutrition. *The American Journal of Clinical Nutrition.* 1998;68(1):126-133.

*Journal of the American Academy of Dermatology,* Volume 52, Number 3, March 2005.

*The Journal of Nutritional Biochemistry.* 2006. Feb;17(2):117-25.

Masaki, H. Role of antioxidants in the skin: anti-aging effects. *J Dermatol.* 2010 May;58(2):85-90.

Nichols, JA, Katiyar, SK. Skin photoprotection by natural polyphenols: anti-inflammatory, antioxidant and DNA mechanisms.

*Arch Dermatol Res.* 2010 Mar;302(2):71-83.

Srikanth, V, Maczurek, A. et al. Advanced glycation end products and their receptor RAGE in Alzheimer's disease, *Neurobiology of aging* 32 (5) 763–77 (2011)

Simm, A, Wagner, J. et al. Advanced glycation endproducts: a biomarker for age as an outcome predictor after cardiac surgery? *Experimental gerontology* 42 (7) 668–75 (2007)

Wickett, R. et al. Effect of Oral Intake of Choline-Stabilized Orthosilicic Acid on Hair Tensile Strength and Morphology in Women with Fine Hair. *Archives of Dermatological Research*, Volume 299, 2007.

## Chapter 3: Collagen and Bones

Bischoff-Ferrari HA, Dawson-Hughes B, Baron JA, et al. Calcium intake and hip fracture risk in men and women: a meta-analysis of prospective cohort studies and randomized controlled trials. *Am J Clin Nutr.* 2007; 86:1780–90.

Feskanich D, Willett WC, Stampfer MJ, Colditz GA. Milk, dietary calcium, and bone fractures in women: a 12-year prospective study. *Am J Public Health.* 1997; 87:992–97.

Melton L, Thamer M, Ray N, et al. Fractures attributable to osteoporosis: report from the National Osteoporosis Foundation. *Journal of Bone and Mineral Research.* 1997;12: 16-23

Owusu W, Willett WC, Feskanich D, Ascherio A, Spiegelman D, Colditz GA. Calcium intake and the incidence of forearm and hip fractures among men. *J Nutr.* 1997; 127:1782–87.

Shuster, S. Osteoporosis, a unitary hypothesis of collagen loss in skin and bone. *Med Hypotheses.* 2005;65(3):426-32.

Spector, T. et al. Effect on Bone Turnover and BMD of Low Dose Oral Silicon as an Adjunct to Calcium/Vitamin D3 in a Randomized, Placebo-Controlled Trial. *Journal of Bone and Mineral Research.* 2005. Volume 20. Supplement 1.

Spector, T. et al. Choline-stabilized Orthosilicic acid supplementation as an adjunct to calcium/vitamin D3 stimulates Markers of bone formation in osteopenic Females: a randomized, placebo-controlled trial. *BMC Musculoskeletal Disorders.* 2008. Volume 9. Number 85

Viguet-Carrin, S. et al. The Role of Collagen in Bone Strength. *Osteoporosis Int.* 2006;17:319-336.

## Chapter 4: Collagen and Joints

Arora R, Basu N, Kapoor V, et al. Anti-inflammatory studies on Curcuma longa (turmeric). *Ind J Med Res* 1971;59:1289-1295.

Chandra D, Gupta S. Anti-inflammatory and anti-arthritic activity of volatile oil of *Curcuma longa* (Haldi). *Ind J Med Res* 1972;60:138-142.

Geusens P. et al., Presentation at EULAR 2014, *Annals of Rheumatic Diseases – the EULAR Journal.*

Heidary B, Heidari P, el al. Association between serum vitamin

D deficiency and knee osteoarthritis. *Internal Orthopaedics.* 2011 Nov; 35(11): 1627-1631.

Jurenka, JA. Anti-inflammatory properties of curcumin, a major constituent of Curcuma longa; a review of preclinical and clinical research. *Alternative Medicine Review.* 2009 June;14(2): 141-153.

McAlindon TE, Felson DT, et al. Relation of dietary intake and serum levels of vitamin D to progression of osteoarthritis of the knees among participants in the Framingham Study. Annals of Internal Medicine. 1996;125:353-359.

Mukhopadhyay A, Basu N, Ghatak N, et al. Anti-inflammatory and irritant activities of curcumin analogues in rats. *Agents Actions* 1982;12:508-515.

Peregoy J, Wilder FV. The effects of vitamin C supplementation on incident and progressive knee osteoarthritis: a longitudinal study. *Public Health Nutrition* 2011 Apr;14(4):709-715.

## Chapter 5: Collagen and Cardiovascular Disease

Boonmark NW; Lou XJ; Yang ZJ; Schwartz K; Zhang JL; Rubin EM; Lawn RM. Modification of apolipoprotein(a) lysine binding site reduces atherosclerosis in transgenic mice. *J Clin Invest* 1997 Aug 1;100(3):558-64.

Gauthier GM, Keevil JG, McBride PE. The association of homocysteine and coronary artery disease. Clinical Cardiology 2003;26:563-568.

Go AS, Mozaffarian D, Roger VL, Benjamin EJ, Berry JD, Blaha

MJ, et al. Heart disease and stroke statistics—2014 update: a report from the American Heart Association. *Circulation.* 2014 ;128.

Heidenreich PA, Trogdon JG, Khavjou OA, et al. Forecasting the future of cardiovascular disease in the United States: a policy statement from the American Heart Association. *Circulation.* 2011;123:933-44. Epub 2011 Jan 24.

Murphy SL, Xu JQ, Kochanek KD. Deaths: Final data for 2010. *Natl Vital Stat Rep.* 2013;61(4).

www.paulingtherapy.com

Yang, Q, Zhang, Z, Gregg, EW et al. Added sugar intake and cardiovascular diseases mortality among US adults. *JAMA Intern Med.* 2014 Apr;174(4):516-24

## Chapter 6: Collagen and Stress

Houck JC, Sharma VK, Patel YM, Gladner JA (October 1968). "Induction of collagenolytic and proteolytic activities by anti-inflammatory drugs in the skin and fibroblast". *Biochem. Pharmacol.* 17 (10): 2081–90

Kucharz EJ (1988). "Hormonal control of collagen metabolism. Part II". *Endocrinologie* 26 (4): 229–37.

Simmons PS, Miles JM, Gerich JE, Haymond MW (February 1984). "Increased proteolysis. An effect of increases in plasma cortisol within the physiologic range". *J. Clin. Invest.* 73 (2): 412–20.

## Chapter 7: Collagen and Menopause

Calleja-Agius J, Muscat-Baron Y, Brincat MP. Skin ageing. *Menopause Int.* 2007 Jun;13(2):60-4.

Philp, HA. Hot Flashes – A Review of the Literature on Alternative and Complementary Treatment Approaches. *Alternative Medicine Review.* Volume 8, Number 3. 2002.

Stevenson S, Thornton J. Effect of estrogens on skin aging and the potential role of SERMs. *Clin Interv Aging.* 2007;2(3):283-97.

Stolze H. An alternative to treat menopausal symptoms with a phytotherapeutic agent. *Med Welt.* 1985 36:871:74.

## Chapter 8: Collagen and Environmental Toxins

Centre for health, environment and justice www.chej.org

Csaba, Leranth et al. Bisphenol A prevents the synaptogenic response to estradiol in hippocampus and prefrontal cortex of ovariectomized nonhuman primates. *Hormones and Cancer.* Published September 3, 2008.

Harley, Kim G. et al. Prenatal and early childhood bisphenol A concentrations and behavior in school-aged children. *Environmental Research.* Volume 126, October 2013, Pages 43–50

Machtinger, Ronit et al. Bisphenol-A and human oocyte maturation *in vitro Hum. Reprod.* first published online July 30, 2013

World Health Organization www.who.int/en/

www.safespaceprotection.com
www.saferchemicals.org
www.ewg.org

# Thank you!

Thank you for picking up a copy of *"Collagen - Myths and Misconceptions"*. I have the pleasure of working with people every day and helping them navigate life's choices, so they can feel vibrant and healthy and live each day to the fullest. I pursued a career in Naturopathic Medicine 10+ years ago because I believe that "health is wealth" and truly great health begins with education, lifestyle changes and preventing disease, not suppressing symptoms.

Begin today, it's never too late to start eating healthy and exercising which will make your life more rewarding, because you'll be able to do anything and everything you want to. You won't ever regret taking simple steps to health and wellness. Many of the issues that affect huge segments of our population can be completely reversed and prevented with a healthy diet, lifestyle changes and learning how to cope with stress, by turning stress into a challenge that YOU can overcome.

Sharing my passion for health and motivating people to make positive changes with their health is the greatest gift I can offer. Visit my website at *www.doctormarita.com* and sign up for my FREE newsletter. I love to share recipes, exercise and lifestyle tips to enhance your mind, body and spirit.

*Here's to challenges and your vibrant health,*
Dr Marita

## doctormarita.com

  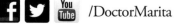 /DoctorMarita